Coles Notes
Study Guide
Economics

John Wiley & Sons Canada, Ltd.

Coles Notes Study Guide Economics
Published by:
John Wiley & Sons Canada, Ltd.
6045 Freemont Blvd.
Mississauga, Ontario
L5R 4J3

Copyright © 2012 John Wiley & Sons Canada, Ltd.

ISBN: 978-1-118-30736-6

Printed in Canada

1 2 3 4 5 WEB 16 15 14 13 12

Table of Contents

INTRODUCTION

What is economics? Economics is the study of how society allocates scarce resources and goods. Resources are the inputs that society uses to produce output, called goods. Resources include inputs such as labour, capital, and land. Goods include products such as food, clothing, and housing as well as services such as those provided by barbers, doctors, and police officers. These resources and goods are considered scarce because of society's tendency to demand more resources and goods than are available.

While most resources and goods are scarce, some are not—for example, the air that we breathe. A resource or good that is not scarce, even when its price is zero, is called a **free** resource or good. Economics, however, is mainly concerned with **scarce** resources and goods. It is the presence of **scarcity** that motivates the study of how society allocates resources and goods.

One means by which society allocates scarce resources and goods is the market system. The term **market** refers to any arrangement that allows people to trade with one another. The **market system** is the name given to the collection of all markets and also refers to the relationships among these markets. The study of the market system, which is the subject of economics, is divided into two main branches or theories; they are **macroeconomics** and **microeconomics.**

Macroeconomics

The prefix *macro* means large, indicating that **macroeconomics** is concerned with the study of the market system on a large scale. Macroeconomics considers the **aggregate** performance of *all* markets in the market system and is concerned with the choices made by the large subsectors of the economy—the household sector, which includes all consumers; the business sector, which includes all firms; and the government sector, which includes all government agencies.

Microeconomics

The prefix micro means small, indicating that **microeconomics** is concerned with the study of the market system on a small scale. Microeconomics looks at the **individual markets** that make up the market system and is concerned with the choices made by small economic units such as individual consumers, individual firms, or individual government agencies.

Economic Policy

An **economic policy** is a course of action that is intended to influence or control the behaviour of the economy. Economic policies are typically implemented and administered by the government. Examples of economic policies include decisions made about government spending and taxation, about the redistribution of income from rich to poor, and about the supply of money. The effectiveness of economic policies can be assessed in one of two ways, known as **positive** and **normative** economics.

Positive and normative economics. Positive economics attempts to describe how the economy and economic policies work without re-sorting to value judgments about which results are best. The distinguishing feature of positive economic hypotheses is that they *can be tested* and either confirmed or rejected. For example, the hypothesis that "an increase in the supply of money leads to an increase in prices" belongs to the realm of positive economics because it can be tested by examining the data on the supply of money and the level of prices.

Normative economics involves the use of **value judgments** to assess the performance of the economy and economic policies. Consequently, normative economic hypotheses *cannot be tested*. For example, the hypothesis that "the inflation rate is too high" belongs to the realm of normative economics because it is based on a value judgment and therefore cannot be tested, confirmed, or refuted. Not surprisingly, most of the disagreements among economists concern normative economic hypotheses.

Goals of economic policy. The goals of economic policy consist of value judgments about what economic policy should strive to achieve and therefore fall under the heading of normative economics. While there is much disagreement about the appropriate goals of economic policy, several appear to have wide, although not universal, acceptance. These widely accepted goals include:

1. **Economic growth:** Economic growth means that the incomes of all consumers and firms (after accounting for inflation) are increasing over time.

2. **Full employment:** The goal of full employment is that every member of the labour force who wants to work is able to find work.

3. **Price stability:** The goal of price stability is to prevent increases in the general price level known as **inflation,** as well as decreases in the general price level known as **deflation.**

Economic Analysis

Economic analysis is **marginal analysis.** In marginal analysis, one examines the consequences of adding to or subtracting from the current state of affairs. Consider, for example, an employer's decision to hire a new worker. The employer must determine the **marginal benefit** of hiring the additional worker as well as the **marginal cost.** The marginal benefit of hiring the worker is the value of the additional goods or services that the new worker could produce. The marginal cost is the additional wages the employer will have to pay the new worker. An economic analysis of the decision to hire the new worker involves weighing the marginal benefits against the marginal costs. If the marginal benefits are greater than the marginal costs, then it makes sense for the employer to hire the worker. If not, then the new worker should not be hired.

Ceteris paribus **assumption.** In performing economic analysis, it is sometimes difficult to separate out the effects of different factors on decisions or outcomes. For example, the decision of students to attend university may depend on a number of factors, including income, the tuition charged, or the market value of a university degree. The effect of an increase in tuition on university enrollment may not be immediately apparent because student incomes or the market value of a university degree may be changing along with the increase in tuition. To conduct a proper economic analysis of the effect of a rise in tuition on university enrollment requires that all other factors affecting the decision to attend university be held constant. The assumption of *ceteris paribus,* which is

Latin for "all else held constant," is frequently invoked in economic analysis. The phrase *ceteris paribus* conveys the assumption that only one of many factors is being examined. For example, if an increase in tuition led to a decrease in university enrollment taking into account all other factors such as changes in student incomes or in the market value of a university degree, one could summarize this finding with the statement: an increase in tuition reduces university enrollment, *ceteris paribus*.

Efficient production and the production possibilities frontier. In addition to the *ceteris paribus* assumption, economic analysis is often carried out under the assumption of **efficient production.** According to the efficient production assumption, the economy is always using its resources and technology to produce the *maximum* number of goods possible.

The efficient production assumption is frequently associated with the **production possibilities frontier (PPF),** a graphical device that is used for economic analysis of production decisions. The PPF measures the quantity of two goods that an economy is capable of producing with its currently available resources and technology. While economies typically produce more than two goods, the graphical analysis of the PPF is made easier by restricting the production possibilities of the economy to just two goods.

Figure 1 A production possibilities frontier

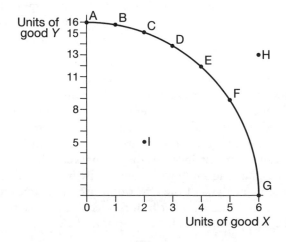

Figure 1 depicts a PPF for an economy that is producing the goods X and Y. The PPF is the curved line through points A, B, C, D, E, F, and G. It represents the maximum possible quantities of goods X and Y that the economy is capable of producing and therefore symbolizes the efficient production assumption. The quantity of good X produced is measured on the horizontal axis, while the quantity of good Y produced is measured on the vertical axis. At point A on the PPF, the economy is using all of its resources to produce 16 units of good Y and 0 units of good X. Moving down along the PPF to the right of point A, fewer units of Y are produced, and more and more units of X are produced. At point B, the economy is producing 15 units of Y and 1 unit of X; at point C, the economy is producing 13 units of Y and 2 units of X, and so on. When the economy is producing at point G, it is putting all of its resources into production of good X—6 units of good X and 0 units of good Y. Points that lie in the interior of the curved PPF, such as point I, represent quantities of goods X and Y that are less than the maximum quantities the economy is capable of producing and are therefore considered **inefficient production points.** Under the efficient production assumption, production quantities such as point I can be excluded from any economic analysis. Because the PPF curve represents the maximum possible quantities of goods X and Y that the economy is capable of producing, points that lie beyond the PPF, such as point H, represent **unattainable production points** and can also be ruled out.

The bowed-out, concave shape of the PPF is due to the presumption that the economy's resources are not equally well suited to the production of both goods X and Y. For example, some resources may not be very useful in producing good X but are very useful in producing good Y. If the economy were initially using *all* of its resources to produce 6 units of X—point G on the PPF—but then decided to produce 1 less unit of good X—5 units of X—some of the resources that are better suited to producing good Y would be released with the result that 5 units of good Y could now be produced—point F on the PPF. If the economy decided to produce only 4 units of good X, then even more resources would be released, and 3 more units of good Y, for a total of 8 units of good Y, could now be produced—point E on the PPF.

A special case arises when the resources used to produce good Y are *equally well suited* for the production of good X. In this case, the PPF would not be curved outward. Instead, the PPF would simply be a straight line connecting the points where the economy is using all of its resources to produce good Y (point A) and where the economy is using all of its resources to produce good X (point G).

It is important to note that the PPF drawn in Figure 1 depicts production possibilities for **fixed resources** and **fixed technology.** If the amount of resources available to produce goods X and Y were to increase as a result of economic growth, then the PPF curve would shift outward, to the right, implying that the economy could produce greater quantities of both goods X and Y. The same holds true when improvements in technology allow for more efficient use of available resources; the PPF will shift outward, to the right. Production points such as point H may then become attainable.

Opportunity cost. In addition to displaying the economy's efficient production possibilities, the PPF is also used to illustrate an important concept in economic analysis called **opportunity cost.** The opportunity cost of a decision or choice that one makes is the value of the **highest valued alternative** that could have been chosen but was instead foregone. For example, suppose that one is faced with several ways of spending an evening at home. The choice made is to study economics (perhaps because there is an economics test tomorrow). The opportunity cost of this choice is the value of the highest valued alternative to the time spent studying economics. While there may be many alternatives to studying economics—watching television, reading a novel, talking on the telephone—there is only one alternative that has highest value. In this example, the alternative with highest value depends on one's own preferences. The value of the highest valued alternative—say, for example, reading a novel—would be considered the opportunity cost of studying economics.

The concept of opportunity cost also applies to production decisions. Returning to the PPF in Figure 1, suppose that the economy is initially at point C, producing 2 units of good X and 13 units of good Y. Consider what happens when the economy desires another unit of good X and so changes its production from point C on the PPF to point D. The opportunity cost of the additional unit of good X is the 2 units of good Y (13 units of Y – 11 units of Y) that are foregone in moving from point C to point D. In the case of the PPF, where there are only two goods, the highest valued alternative to good X is good Y and vice versa.

Now, suppose that the economy desires yet another unit of good X and so changes its production from point D on the PPF to point E. The opportunity cost of this additional unit of good X is now 3 units of good Y (11 units of Y – 8 units of Y). In this example, the opportunity cost of producing 1 more unit of good X increases as more of good X is produced. The reason is that some of the resources used to produce good Y are not as well suited to producing good X. (You should recall that this is the same reason for the bowed-out, concave shape of the PPF.) Consequently, as more and more of the economy's resources are devoted to producing good X, the opportunity cost of good X, as measured in units of good Y foregone, will be increasing. This phenomenon is referred to as the **law of increasing opportunity cost.**

Common pitfalls in economic analysis. There are two "pitfalls" that should be avoided when conducting economic analysis: the **fallacy of composition** and the **false-cause fallacy.** The fallacy of composition is the belief that if one individual or firm benefits from some action, all individuals or all firms will benefit from the same action. While this may in fact be the case, it is *not necessarily so.* For example, suppose an airline decides to lower the fares it charges on all of its routes. The airline expects to benefit from the fare reduction because it believes the lower fares will attract customers away from other airlines. If, however, the other airlines follow suit and lower their airfares by the same amount, then it is not necessarily true that all airlines will be better off: while more people may choose to fly, each airline will receive less money per passenger, and each airline's market share is unlikely to change. Hence, the profits of all airlines could fall.

The false-cause fallacy often arises in economic analysis of two correlated actions or events. When one observes that two actions or events seem to be correlated, it is often tempting to conclude that one event has caused the other. But by doing so, one may be committing the false-cause fallacy, which is the simple fact that *correlation does not imply causation.* For example, suppose that new-car prices have steadily increased over some period of time and that new-car sales have also increased over this same period. One might then conclude that an increase in the price of new cars causes an increase in new-car sales. This false conclusion is an example of the false-cause fallacy; new-car prices and new-car sales may be positively correlated, but that correlation does not imply that there is any causation between the two. In order to explain why both events are taking place simultaneously, one may have to look at other factors—for example, rising consumer incomes, inflation, or rising producer costs.

Chapter 1

DEMAND, SUPPLY, AND ELASTICITY

In every market, there are both buyers and sellers. The buyers' willingness to buy a particular good (at various prices) is referred to as the buyers' demand for that good. The sellers' willingness to supply a particular good (at various prices) is referred to as the sellers' supply of that good.

Demand

The buyers' demand is represented by a demand schedule, which lists the quantities of a good that buyers are willing to purchase at different prices. An example of a demand schedule for a certain good X is given in Table 1-1. Note that as the price of good X *increases*, the quantity demanded of good X *decreases*.

Table 1-1   Demand Schedule For Good X

Price of good X	Quantity demanded
$0	5
2	4
4	3
6	2
8	1
10	0

This kind of behaviour on the part of buyers is in accordance with the law of demand. According to the law of demand, an inverse relationship exists between the price of a good and the quantity demanded of that good. As the price of a good goes up, buyers demand less of that good. This inverse relationship is more readily seen using the graphical device known as the demand curve, which is nothing more than a graph of the demand schedule. A demand curve for the demand schedule given in Table 1-1 is presented in Figure 1-1.

Figure 1-1 Demand curve for good *X*

The vertical axis in Figure 1-1 depicts the price per unit of good *X* measured in dollars, while the horizontal axis depicts the quantity demanded of good *X* measured in units of good *X*. In addition to the demand schedule and the demand curve, the buyers' demand for a good can also be expressed a third way—algebraically, using a **demand equation.** The demand equation relates the price of the good, denoted by *P*, to the quantity of the good demanded, denoted by *Q*. For example, the demand equation for good *X* corresponding to the demand schedule in Table 1 and the demand curve in Figure 1-1 is

$$P = 10 - 2Q$$

From the demand equation, you can determine the **intercept** value where the quantity demanded is zero, as well as the **slope** of the demand curve. In the example above, the intercept value is 10 and the slope of the demand curve is −2. In order to satisfy the law of demand, the slope of the demand equation must be *negative* so that there is an inverse relationship between the price and quantity demanded.

Change in the quantity demanded. A **change in the quantity demanded** is a *movement along the demand curve* due to a change in the **price** of the good being demanded. As an example, suppose that in Figure 1-1 the current market price charged for good X is $4 so that the current quantity demanded of good X is 3 units. If the price of good X increases to $6, the quantity demanded of good X moves along the demand curve to the left, resulting in new quantity demanded of 2 units of good X. The change in the quantity demanded due to the $2 increase in the price of good X is *1 less unit of good X*. Similarly, a decrease in the price of good X from $4 to $2 would induce a movement along the demand curve to the right, and the change in the quantity demanded would be 1 more unit of good X.

Change in demand. A **change in demand** is represented *by a shift of the demand curve.* As a result of this shift, the quantity demanded at all prices will have changed. Figures 1-2(a) and 1-2(b) present just two of the many possible ways in which the demand curve for good X might shift. In both figures, the original demand curve is the same as in Figure 1-1 and is denoted by D_A. In Figure 1-2(a), demand curve D_A has shifted to the *left* to the new demand curve D_B. The leftward shift means that at all possible prices, the demand for good X will be *less* than before. For example, before the shift, a price of $4 corresponded to a quantity demanded of 3 units of good X. After the shift left, at the same price of $4, the quantity demanded is less, at 1 unit of good X. In Figure 1-2(b), demand curve D_A has shifted to the *right* to the new demand curve D_C. The rightward shift means that at all possible prices, the demand for good X will be greater than before. For example, before the shift, a price of $6 implied a quantity demanded of 2 units of good X. After the shift, at the same price of $6, the quantity demanded is greater, at 4 units of good X.

Figure 1-2   A change in demand: Leftward and rightward shifts of the demand curve for good *X*

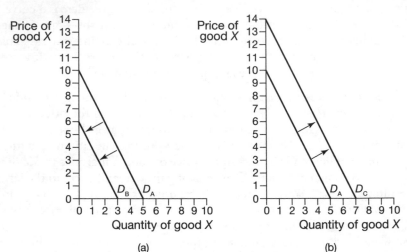

(a)   (b)

Reasons for a change in demand. It is important to keep straight the difference between a change in quantity demanded, or a movement *along* the demand curve, and a change in demand, or *shift* in the demand curve. There is only *one* reason for a change in the quantity demanded of good *X:* a change in the price of good *X;* however, there are several reasons for a *change in demand for good X,* including:

1. **Changes in the price of related goods:** The demand for good *X* may be changed by increases or decreases in the prices of other, *related* goods. These related goods are usually divided into two categories called **substitutes** and **complements.** *A substitute* for good *X* is any good *Y* that satisfies most of the same needs as good *X.* For example, if good *X* is butter, a substitute good *Y* might be margarine. When two goods *X* and *Y* are substitutes, then as the price of the substitute good *Y rises,* the demand for good *X increases* and the demand curve for good *X* shifts to the *right,* as in Figure 1-2(b). Conversely, as the price of the substitute good *Y falls,* the demand for good *X decreases* and the demand curve for good *X* shifts to the *left,* as in Figure 1-2(a). *A complement to* good *X* is any good that is consumed in some proportion to good *X.* For example, if good *X* is a pair of shoelaces, then a complement good *Y* might be a pair of shoes. When two goods *X* and *Y* are complements, then as the price

of the complementary good *Y rises*, the demand for good *X decreases* and the demand curve for good *X* shifts to the *left*, as in Figure 1-2(a). Conversely, as the price of the complementary good *Y falls*, the demand for good *X increases* and the demand curve for good *X* shifts to the *right*, as in Figure 1-2(b).

2. **Changes in income:** The demand for good *X* may also be affected by changes in the **incomes** of buyers. Typically, as incomes *rise*, the demand for a good will usually *increase* at all prices and the demand curve will shift to the *right*, as in Figure 1-2(b). Similarly, when incomes *fall*, the demand for a good will *decrease* at all prices and the demand curve will shift to the *left*, as in Figure 1-2(a). Goods for which changes in demand vary directly with changes in income are called **normal** goods. There are some goods, however, for which an *increase* in income leads to *a decrease* in demand and a *decrease* in income leads to an *increase* in demand. Goods for which changes in demand vary inversely with changes in income are called **inferior** goods. For example, consider the two goods meat and potatoes. As incomes increase, people demand relatively more meat and relatively fewer potatoes, implying that meat may be regarded as a normal good, and potatoes may be considered an inferior good.

3. **Changes in preferences:** As peoples' preferences for goods and services change over time, the demand curve for these goods and services will also shift. For example, as the price of gasoline has risen, automobile buyers have demanded more fuel-efficient, "economy" cars and fewer gas-guzzling, "luxury" cars. This change in preferences could be illustrated by a shift to the right in the demand curve for economy cars and a shift to the left in the demand curve for luxury cars.

4. **Changes in expectations:** Demand curves may also be shifted by changes in expectations. For example, if buyers expect that they will have a job for many years to come, they will be more willing to purchase goods such as cars and homes that require payments over a long period of time, and therefore, the demand curves for these goods will shift to the right. If buyers fear losing their jobs, perhaps because of a recessionary economic climate, they will demand fewer goods requiring long-term payments and will therefore cause the demand curves for these goods to shift to the left.

Supply

The buyers' demand for goods is not the only factor determining market prices and quantities. The sellers' **supply** of goods also plays a role in determining market prices and quantities. Like the buyers' demand, the sellers supply can be represented in three different ways: by a **supply schedule,** by a **supply curve,** and **algebraically.** An example of a supply schedule for a certain good *X* is given in Table 1-2, and the corresponding supply curve is drawn in Figure 1-3. Note that as the price of good *X* *increases,* the quantity supplied of good *X increases.* This kind of behaviour on the part of sellers is in accordance with the **law of supply.**

Table 1-2   Supply Schedule for Good *X*

Price of good X	Quantity supplied
$0	0
1	2
2	4
3	6
4	8
5	10

Figure 1-3   Supply curve for good *X*

According to the law of supply, a **direct relationship** exists between the price of a good and the quantity supplied of that good. As the price of a good increases, sellers are willing to supply more of that good. The law of supply is also reflected in the upward-sloping supply curve of Figure 1-3 and in the algebraic equation of the supply schedule data of Table 1-2:

$$P = \frac{1}{2}Q$$

which has a *positive* slope of $\frac{1}{2}$.

Change in the quantity supplied. A **change in the quantity supplied** is *a movement along the supply curve* due to a change in the **price** of the good supplied. Suppose, in Figure 1-3, the price changes from $4 to $3. The change in the quantity supplied is found by moving along the supply curve, in this case to the left, from the old quantity of 8 units of good X *to* the new quantity of 6 units of good X.

Change in supply. A **change in supply,** like a change in demand, is represented by a *shift in the supply curve.* Figures 1-4(a) and 1-4(b) illustrate two possible ways in which the supply curve for good X might shift:

Figure 1-4   A change in supply: Leftward and rightward shifts of the supply curve for good X

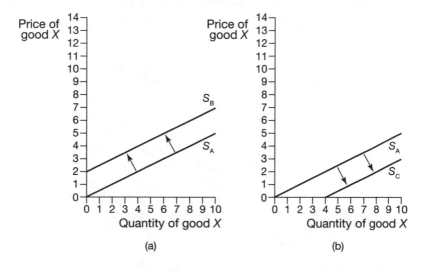

(a)   (b)

A *leftward shift* of the original supply curve, labeled S_A, to the new supply curve S_B, as depicted in Figure 1-4(a), results in a **reduced supply** of good X at all prices. *A rightward shift* of the original supply curve S_A to the new supply curve S_C, as depicted in Figure 1-4(b), results in an **increased supply** of good X at all prices.

Reasons for a change in supply. A change in supply or shift of the supply curve is not caused by a change in the price of the good being supplied; that would induce a change in the quantity demanded and a movement along the supply curve. A shift in the supply curve is caused by other factors, including:

1. **Changes in the prices of other goods:** Suppliers are frequently able to switch their production processes from one type of good to another. Farmers, for example, might decide to grow less wheat and more corn on the same land if the price of corn rises relative to the price of wheat. In this case, the supply curve for wheat would shift to the *left,* as in Figure 1-4(a), as a consequence of the higher price for corn.

2. **Changes in the prices of inputs:** The prices of the raw materials or inputs used to produce a good also cause the supply curve to shift. An *increase* in the prices of a good's inputs will *raise* costs to suppliers and cause suppliers to supply *less* of that good at all prices. Therefore, an *increase* in the prices of a good's inputs leads to *a leftward shift* of the supply curve for that good, as in Figure 1-4(a). A *decrease* in the prices of a good's inputs *reduces* costs and allows suppliers to supply more of that good at all prices. Therefore, a *decrease* in the prices of a good's inputs leads to a *rightward shift* of the supply curve for that good, as in Figure 1-4(b).

3. **Changes in technology:** Advances in technology often have the effect of lowering the costs of production, allowing suppliers to supply more goods at all prices. For example, the development of pesticides has reduced the amount of damage done to certain crops and therefore has reduced the cost of farming. The result has been an increase in the supply of these crops at all prices, which can be represented by a shift to the right in the supply curves for these crops, as in Figure 1-4(b).

Equilibrium Analysis

The previous two sections have examined the demand decisions of buyers and the supply decisions of sellers, *separately*. However, in the market for any particular good *X,* the decisions of buyers *interact simultaneously* with the decisions of sellers. When the demand for good *X* equals the supply of good *X,* the market for good *X* is said to be in **equilibrium.** Associated with any market equilibrium will be an **equilibrium quantity** and an **equilibrium price.** The equilibrium quantity of good *X* is that quantity for which the quantity demanded of good *X* exactly equals the quantity supplied of good *X.* The equilibrium price for good *X* is that price per unit of good *X* that allows the market to "clear"; that is, the price for which the quantity demanded of good *X* exactly equals the quantity supplied of good *X.* The determination of equilibrium quantity and price, known as **equilibrium analysis,** can be achieved in two different ways: by simultaneously solving the algebraic equations for demand and supply or by combining the demand and supply curves in a single graph and determining the equilibrium price and quantity graphically.

The algebraic approach to equilibrium. The algebraic approach to equilibrium analysis is to solve, simultaneously, the algebraic equations for demand and supply. In the example given above, the demand equation for good *X* was

$$P = 10 - 2Q$$

and the supply equation for good *X* was

$$P = \frac{1}{2}Q$$

To solve simultaneously, one first rewrites either the demand or the supply equation as a function of price. In the example above, the supply curve may be rewritten as follows:

$$Q = 2P$$

Substituting this expression into the demand equation, one can solve for the equilibrium price:

$$P = 10 - 2(2P)$$
$$\rightarrow P = 10 - 4P$$
$$\rightarrow 5P = 10$$
$$\rightarrow \quad P = 2$$

The equilibrium price of good X is found to be \$2. Substituting the equilibrium price of 2 into the rewritten supply equation for good X, one has:

$$Q = 2(2)$$
$$\rightarrow Q = 4$$

The equilibrium quantity is found to be 4 units of good X.

A graphical depiction of equilibrium. The graphical approach to equilibrium analysis is illustrated in Figure 1-5, which combines the demand and supply curves of Figures 1-1 and 1-3 into a single graph. The equilibrium price and quantity are determined by the intersection of the two curves. The equilibrium quantity is 4 units of good X, and the equilibrium price is \$2 per unit of good X. This result is the same as the one obtained by simultaneously solving the algebraic equations for demand and supply.

Figure 1-5   Equilibrium in the market for good X

A price of \$2 and a quantity of 4 units of X are the equilibrium price and quantity only when the demand and supply for good X are exactly as depicted in Figure 1-5. If either the demand curve or the supply curve shifts, the equilibrium price and quantity change. Examples of shifts in the demand and supply curves and the resultant changes in equilibrium are illustrated in Figures 1-6(a) and 1-6(b). In Figure 1-6(a), a shift to *left* of the *demand* curve, from D_A to D_B, leads to *a decrease* in *both* the equilibrium price and quantity of good X, while a shift to the right of the demand curve, from D_A to D_C, leads to an *increase* in *both* the equilibrium price and quantity of good X, assuming supply is held constant—the *ceteris paribus* assumption. In Figure 1-6(b), a shift to the *left* of the *supply* curve, from S_A to S_B, leads to an increase in the equilibrium price of good X but *a decrease* in the equilibrium quantity of good X, assuming demand is held constant. A shift to the *right* of the supply curve, *from S_A to S_C*, leads to *a decrease* in the equilibrium price of good X but an *increase* in the equilibrium quantity of good X, again assuming that demand is held constant.

Figure 1-6   Changes in Equilibrium

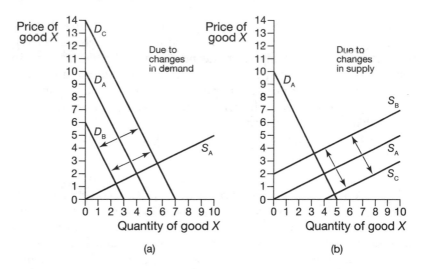

(a)   (b)

Elasticity

In addition to understanding how equilibrium prices and quantities change as demand and supply change, economists are also interested in understanding how demand and supply change in response to changes in prices and incomes. The responsiveness of demand or supply to changes in prices or incomes is measured by the **elasticity** of demand or supply.

Price elasticity of demand and supply. The **price elasticity of demand** is given by the formula:

$$\text{price elasticity of demand} = \frac{\text{percentage change in quantity demanded}}{\text{percentage change in price}}$$

The **price elasticity of supply** is given by a similar formula:

$$\text{price elasticity of supply} = \frac{\text{percentage change in quantity supplied}}{\text{percentage change in price}}$$

If the percentage change in quantity demanded is *greater* than the percentage change in price, demand is said to be **price elastic,** or very responsive to price changes. If the percentage change in quantity demanded is *less* than the percentage change in price, demand is said to be **price inelastic,** or not very responsive to price changes. Similarly, supply is price elastic when the percentage change in quantity supplied is greater than the percentage change in price, and supply is price inelastic when the percentage change in quantity supplied is less than the percentage change in price.

The price elasticity of demand or supply will *differ* among goods. For example, consider a 50 per cent increase in the price of two goods—candy bars and prescription medicines. While the demand for both candy bars and prescription medicines should decline in response to the price increases, the percentage change in the quantity demanded of candy bars is likely to be much greater than the percentage change in the quantity demanded of prescription medicines because candy bars are less of a necessity than prescription medicines. You could summarize this finding by stating that the demand for candy bars is more price *elastic* than the demand for prescription medicines. Alternatively, you might state that the demand for prescription medicines is more price *inelastic* than the demand for candy bars.

Two extreme cases. There are two cases where the price elasticity of demand or supply can take on extreme values. One is the case of **perfectly price elastic** demand or supply. Demand is perfectly price elastic if for any percentage *decrease* in price, no matter how small, the percentage change in quantity demanded is infinitely large—demanders demand all that they can. Supply is perfectly price elastic if for any percentage *increase* in price, no matter how small, the percentage change in quantity supplied is also infinitely large—suppliers supply all that they can.

The other extreme *case* occurs when the percentage change in quantity demanded or supplied is always equal to 0, regardless of the percentage change in price. In this case, demand or supply is said to be **perfectly price inelastic**, or completely nonresponsive to change in prices.

The two extreme cases are illustrated in Figure 1-7. The demand curve D_1 in Figure 1-7(a) illustrates the case of perfectly price elastic demand, while the supply curve S_1 in Figure 1-7(b) illustrates the case of perfectly price elastic supply. The demand curve D_2 in Figure 1-7(a) illustrates the case of perfectly price inelastic demand, and the supply curve S_2, in Figure 1-7(b) illustrates the case of perfectly price inelastic supply.

Figure 1-7 Perfectly price elastic and perfectly price inelastic demand and supply curves

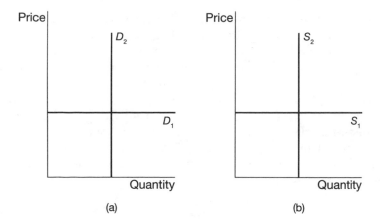

(a) (b)

Income elasticity of demand. The income elasticity of demand is given by the formula:

$$\text{income elasticity of demand} = \frac{\text{percentage change in quantity demanded}}{\text{percentage change in income}}$$

If the percentage change in the quantity demanded is *greater* than the percentage change in income, then demand is said to be **income elastic,** or very responsive to changes in demanders' incomes. If the percentage change in the quantity demanded is *less* than the percentage change in income, then demand is said to be **income inelastic,** or not very responsive to changes in demanders' incomes. Notice from the definition of income elasticity that if the income elasticity of demand is *positive,* the good must be a *normal good,* and if the income elasticity of demand is *negative,* the good must be an *inferior good.*

Cross-price elasticity of demand. The **cross-price elasticity of demand** is the ratio of the percentage change in the quantity demanded of some good X to a percentage change in the *price of some other good Y.* The cross-price elasticity of demand is given by the formula:

$$\text{cross-price elasticity of demand} = \frac{\text{percentage change in quantity demanded of good } X}{\text{percentage change in price of some other good } X}$$

If the percentage change in the quantity demanded of good X is *greater* than the percentage change in the price of good Y, the demand for good X is **cross-price elastic** with respect to good Y, or very responsive to changes in the price of good Y. If the percentage change in the quantity demanded of good X is *less* than the percentage change in the price of good Y, the demand for good X, is **cross-price inelastic** with respect to good Y, or not very responsive to changes in the price of good Y. From the definition of cross-price elasticity, one may also conclude that if the cross-price elasticity of demand is *positive,* the goods X and Y must be **substitutes,** and if the cross-price elasticity of demand is *negative,* the goods X and Y must be **complements.**

MACROECONOMICS

Chapter 2

GDP, INFLATION, AND UNEMPLOYMENT

The branch of economics known as **macroeconomics** examines the **aggregate** performance of all markets in the market system. In studying macroeconomic behaviour, economists rely on several statistics that measure the performance of the macroeconomy. The three most commonly used measures of macroeconomic performance are the **gross domestic product (GDP)**, the **rate of inflation,** and the **unemployment rate.**

GDP

GDP is defined as the market value of *all* final goods and services produced *domestically* in a single year and is the single most important measure of macroeconomic performance. A related measure of the economy's total output product is **gross national product (GNP),** which is the market value of *all* final goods and services produced by a nation in a single year.

GDP or GNP? The difference between GDP and GNP is rather technical. GDP includes only goods and services produced *within a nation's boundaries.* GNP includes only goods and services produced by *a nation's own citizens and firms.* Goods and services produced outside a nation's boundaries by the nation's own citizens and firms are *included in GNP* but are *excluded from GDP.* Goods and services produced within a nation's boundaries by foreign citizens and firms are *excluded from GNP* but are *included in GDP.* Typically, there is not much difference in the reported values of GDP and GNP; so one may use either statistic to measure overall macroeconomic activity. The rest of this section will therefore focus on GDP.

Measuring GDP: the expenditure and income approaches. There are two ways of measuring GDP, the expenditure approach and the income approach. The **expenditure approach** is to add up the market value of all domestic expenditures made on final goods and services in a single year. **Final goods and services** are goods and services that have been purchased for final use or goods and services that will not be resold or used in production within the year. **Intermediate goods and services,** which are used in the production of final goods and services, are *not included* in the expenditure approach to GDP because expenditures on intermediate goods and services are included in the market value of expenditures made on final goods and services. Including expenditures on both intermediate and final goods and services would lead to **double counting** and an exaggeration of the true market value of GDP.

Total expenditure on final goods and services is broken down into four large expenditure categories, according to the type of good or service purchased. The sum total of these four expenditure categories equals GDP. These *four* expenditure categories are

1. **Consumption expenditures:** Personal consumption expenditures on goods and services comprise the largest share of total expenditure. Consumption *good* expenditures include purchases of **nondurable goods,** such as food and clothing, and purchases of **durable goods,** such as appliances and automobiles. Consumption *service* expenditures include purchases of all kinds of personal services, including those provided by barbers, doctors, lawyers, and mechanics.

2. **Investment expenditures:** Investment expenditures can be divided into two categories: expenditures on **fixed investment goods** and **inventory investment.** Fixed investment goods are those that are useful over a long period of time. Expenditures on *fixed investment goods* include purchases of new equipment, factories, and other nonresidential housing as well as purchases of new residential housing. Also included in fixed investment expenditures is the cost of replacing *existing* investment goods that have become worn out or obsolete. The market value of all investment goods that must be replaced in a single year is referred to as the **depreciation** for that year. *Inventory goods* are final goods waiting to be sold that firms have on hand at the end of the year. The year-to-year change in the market value of firms' inventory goods is considered an investment expenditure because these inventory goods will eventually yield a flow of consumption or production services.

3. **Government expenditures:** Government expenditures on consumption and investment goods and services are treated as a *separate* category in the expenditure approach to GDP. Examples of government expenditures include the hiring of civil servants and military personnel and the construction of roads and public buildings. Social security, welfare, and other **transfer payments** are *not* included in government expenditures. Recipients of transfer payments do not provide any current goods or services in exchanges for these payments. Hence, government expenditures on transfer payments do not involve the purchase of any new goods or services and are therefore excluded from the calculation of government expenditures.

4. **Net exports:** Exports are goods and services produced domestically but sold to foreigners, while **imports** are goods and services produced by foreigners but sold domestically. In the expenditure approach to GDP, expenditures on exports are added to total expenditures, while expenditures on imports are subtracted from total expenditures. Alternatively, one can calculate net exports, which is defined as expenditures on exports minus expenditures on imports, and add the value of net exports to the nation's total expenditures.

The **income approach** to measuring GDP is to add up all the *income* earned by households and firms in a single year. The rationale behind the income *approach* is that total expenditures on final goods and services are eventually received by households and firms in the form of **wage, profit, rent,** and **interest** income. Therefore, by adding together wage, profit, rent, and interest income, one should obtain the same value of GDP as is obtained using the expenditure approach.

There are two types of expenditures, however, that *are included* in the expenditure approach to GDP measurement but *do not* provide households or firms with any form of income: **depreciation expenditures** and **indirect business taxes.** Depreciation expenditures, made to replace existing but deteriorated investment goods, do increase the incomes of those providing the replacement goods, but they also decrease the profit incomes of those purchasing the replacement goods. The result is that aggregate income remains unchanged. Indirect business taxes consist of sales taxes and other excise taxes that firms collect but that are not regarded as a part of firms' incomes. Consequently, indirect business taxes are not included in the income approach to GDP measurement but are included in the expenditure approach.

The difference between the expenditure and income approaches to GDP measurement is illustrated in Figure 2-1.

Figure 2-1   The expenditure and income approaches to GDP measurement

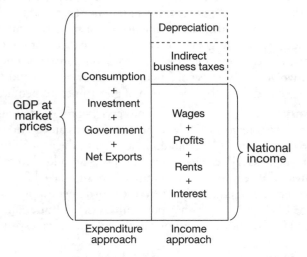

GDP is defined as the total market value of all expenditures made on consumption, investment, government, and net exports in one year. If one subtracts depreciation and indirect business taxes from these expenditures, one arrives at **national income,** which is the sum of all wage, profit, rent, and interest incomes earned in the same year.

Growth rate of GDP. The value of GDP by itself is not very interesting. What is interesting is the **annual growth rate,** or year-to-year percentage change, in the value of GDP. To calculate the percentage change in a statistic, such as GDP, one needs to know the value of the statistic at *two* dates in time. Suppose that the value of GDP last year was Y_L and the value of GDP in the current year is Y_C. Then, the percentage change, or growth rate, of GDP is given by

$$\left[\frac{Y_C - Y_L}{Y_L}\right] \times 100\%$$

This formula is valid for calculating the percentage change in any statistic, not just the percentage change in GDP.

A *positive* growth rate of GDP implies that the economy is expanding, while a *negative* growth rate of GDP implies that the economy is contracting. An expanding economy is said to be in a **boom,** while a contracting economy is said to be in a **recession.**

Nominal GDP, Real GDP, and the Price Level

Nominal GDP is GDP evaluated at current market prices. Therefore, nominal GDP will include all of the changes in market prices that have occurred during the current year due to **inflation** or **deflation.** Inflation is defined as a rise in the overall price level, and deflation is defined as a fall in the overall price level. In order to abstract from changes in the overall price level, another measure of GDP called **real GDP** is often used. Real GDP is GDP evaluated at the *market prices of some base year.* For example, if 1990 were chosen as the base year, then real GDP for 1995 is calculated by taking the quantities of all goods and services purchased in 1995 and multiplying them by their 1990 prices.

GDP deflator. Using the statistics on real GDP and nominal GDP, one can calculate an implicit *index of the price level* for the year. This index is called the **GDP deflator** and is given by the formula

$$\text{GDP deflator} = \frac{\text{nominal GDP}}{\text{real GDP}} \times 100$$

The GDP deflator can be viewed as a **conversion factor** that transforms real GDP into nominal GDP. Note that in the base year, real GDP is by definition equal to nominal GDP so that the GDP deflator in the base year is always equal to 100.

Calculating the rate of inflation or deflation. Suppose that in the year following the base year, the GDP deflator is equal to 110. The **percentage change** in the GDP deflator from the previous (base) year is obtained using the same formula used to calculate the growth rate of GDP. This percentage change is found to be

$$\left[\frac{110 - 100}{100} \right] \times 100\% = 10\%$$

implying that the GDP deflator index has increased 10%. Another way of describing this finding would be to say that the **inflation rate** in the year following the base year was 10%. More generally, if the percentage change in the GDP deflator over some period is a *positive X%,* then the **rate of inflation** over the same period is *X%*. If the percentage change in the GDP deflator over some period is *a negative X%,* then the *rate of deflation* over that period is *X%.*

Consumer price index. The GDP deflator is not the only index measure of the price level. Among the many other price indices, the **consumer price index (CPI)** is the most frequently cited. The CPI differs from the GDP deflator in two important ways. First, the CPI measures only the change in the prices of a "basket" of goods consumed by a typical household. Second, the CPI uses base year quantities rather than current year quantities in calculating the price level index value. The formula for the CPI is given as

$$\text{CPI} = \frac{\text{base year basket quantities multiplied by current year prices}}{\text{base year basket quantities multiplied by base year prices}} \times 100$$

Construction of a price index. As an example of a CPI index, assume for the sake of simplicity that the basket of goods consumed by a typical household consisted of just three goods: pizza, soda, and ice cream. The quantities consumed of each of these three goods in the base year are given in Table 2-1, along with the prices of these three goods in both the base year and the current year.

Table 2-1   Data for a CPI Index

Good	Base year quantity	Base year price	Base year expenditure	Current year price	Current year expenditure
Pizza	12	$11.25	$135.00	$12.00	$144.00
Soda	25	1.55	38.75	1.45	36.25
Ice cream	15	2.95	44.25	3.05	45.75
			$218.00		$226.00

The base year expenditure figures are found by multiplying the *base year quantities* by the *base* year prices. Similarly, the current year expenditure figures are found by multiplying the *base year quantities* by the *current* year prices. In order to calculate a CPI for this basket of three goods, one needs only the total base year and current year expenditures on all three goods. The CPI value for the *current year* may then be calculated as follows:

$$\text{current year CPI} = \left[\frac{226.00}{218.00}\right] \times 100 = 103.67$$

The CPI value for the *base year* is always equal to 100. In this case,

$$\left[\frac{218}{218}\right] \times 100 = 100$$

Thus, the percentage change in the current year CPI from the base year CPI is

$$\text{percentage change in CPI} = \left[\frac{103.67 - 100}{100}\right] \times 100\% = 3.67\%$$

In other words, the *rate of inflation* in the *current year* is 3.67%.

Unemployment Rate

The unemployment rate measures the percentage of the total civilian labour force that are currently unemployed. The formula for the unemployment rate is given by

$$\text{unemployment rate} = \frac{\text{number of people unemployed}}{\text{number of people in the civilian labor force}}$$

The civilian labour force consists of all civilians (non-military personnel), 16 years of age or older, who are willing to work and are not incarcerated. The number of people unemployed is determined according to certain criteria. In the U.S., an unemployed person is a member of the civilian labour force who is currently available for work and who has worked *less than one hour* per week for pay or profit. Furthermore, an unemployed worker must have been actively searching for work during the past month. Workers who are not actively searching for work, referred to as **discouraged workers,** are not considered a part of the civilian labour force and therefore are not counted among the unemployed.

Frictional unemployment. Frictional unemployment is the term used to describe unemployment that results from difficulties in matching *qualified* workers with new jobs. Many qualified workers seeking work are not able to find new jobs right away, usually because of a lack of complete information about new job openings. While it is likely that qualified workers will soon be matched with new jobs, these workers are considered frictionally unemployed during the time that they spend searching for their new jobs.

Structural unemployment. Structural unemployment results from structural changes in the economy that cause workers to lose jobs. The same structural changes also prevent these workers from obtaining new jobs. Structurally unemployed workers are *not qualified* for the new job openings that are available, mainly because they lack the education or training needed for the new jobs. Consequently, the structurally unemployed tend to be out of work for long periods of time, usually until they learn the skills needed for the new jobs or until they decide to relocate.

Chapter 3

AGGREGATE DEMAND AND AGGREGATE SUPPLY

In macroeconomics, the focus is on the demand and supply of *all* goods and services produced by an economy. Accordingly, the demand for all individual goods and services is also combined and referred to as **aggregate demand.** The supply of all individual goods and services is also combined and referred to as **aggregate supply.** Like the demand and supply for individual goods and services, the aggregate demand and aggregate supply for an economy can be represented by a schedule, a curve, or by an algebraic equation.

Aggregate Demand Curve

The **aggregate demand curve** represents the total quantity of all goods (and services) demanded by the economy at different *price levels.* An example of an aggregate demand curve is given in Figure 3-1.

Figure 3-1   An aggregate demand curve

The vertical axis represents the price level of *all* final goods and services. The aggregate price level is measured by either the GDP deflator or the CPI. The horizontal axis represents the real quantity of all goods and services purchased as measured by the level of *real GDP*. Notice that the aggregate demand curve, *AD*, like the demand curves for individual goods, is downward sloping, implying that there is an inverse relationship between the price level and the quantity demanded of real *GDP*.

The reasons for the downward-sloping aggregate demand curve are different from the reasons given for the downward-sloping demand curves for individual goods and services. The demand curve for an individual good is drawn under the assumption that the prices of other goods remain constant and the assumption that buyers' incomes remain constant. As the price of good *X* rises, the demand for good *X* falls because the relative price of other goods is lower and because buyers' real incomes will be reduced if they purchase good *X* at the higher price. The aggregate demand curve, however, is defined in terms of the *price level*. A change in the price level implies that *many* prices are changing, including the wages paid to workers. As wages change, so do incomes. Consequently, it is not possible to assume that prices and incomes remain constant in the construction of the aggregate demand curve. Hence, one cannot explain the downward slope of the aggregate demand curve using the same reasoning given for the downward-sloping individual product demand curves.

Reasons for a downward-sloping aggregate demand curve. Three reasons cause the aggregate demand curve to be downward sloping. The first is the **wealth effect.** The aggregate demand curve is drawn under the assumption that the government holds the **supply of money** constant. One can think of the supply of money as representing the economy's wealth at any moment in time. As the price level *rises,* the wealth of the economy, as measured by the supply of money, declines in value because the purchasing power of money falls. As buyers become poorer, they reduce their purchases of all goods and services. On the other hand, as the price level *falls,* the purchasing power of money rises. Buyers become wealthier and are able to purchase more goods and services than before. The wealth effect, therefore, provides one reason for the inverse relationship between the price level and real GDP that is reflected in the downward-sloping demand curve.

A second reason is the **interest rate effect.** As the price level rises, households and firms require more money to handle their transactions. However, the supply of money is fixed. The increased demand for a fixed supply of money causes the price of money, the **interest rate,** to rise. As the interest rate rises, spending that is sensitive to rate of interest will decline. Hence, the interest rate effect provides another reason for the inverse relationship between the price level and the demand for real GDP.

The third and final reason is the **net exports effect.** As the domestic price level rises, foreign-made goods become relatively cheaper so that the demand for *imports* increases. However, the rise in the domestic price level also means that domestic-made goods are relatively more expensive to foreign buyers so that the demand for *exports* decreases. When exports decrease and imports increase, *net exports* (exports–imports) decrease. Because net exports are a component of real GDP, the demand for real GDP declines as net exports decline.

Changes in aggregate demand. Changes in aggregate demand are represented by shifts of the aggregate demand curve. An illustration of the two ways in which the aggregate demand curve can shift is provided in Figure 3-2.

A shift to the *right* of the aggregate demand curve, from AD_1 to AD_2, means that at the same price levels the quantity demanded of real GDP has *increased.* A shift to the *left* of the aggregate demand curve, from AD_1 to AD_3, means that at the same price levels the quantity demanded of real GDP has *decreased.*

Figure 3-2 Shifts of the aggregate demand curve

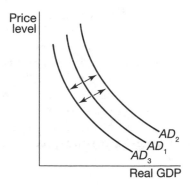

Changes in aggregate demand are *not* caused by changes in the price level. Instead, they are caused by changes in the demand for any of the components of real GDP, changes in the demand for consumption goods and services, changes in investment spending, changes in the government's demand for goods and services, or changes in the demand for net exports.

Consider several examples. Suppose consumers were to decrease their spending on all goods and services, perhaps as a result of a recession. Then, the aggregate demand curve would shift to the left. Suppose interest rates were to fall so that investors increased their investment spending; the aggregate demand curve would shift to the right. If government were to cut spending to reduce a budget deficit, the aggregate demand curve would shift to the left. If the incomes of foreigners were to rise, enabling them to demand more domestic-made goods, net exports would increase, and aggregate demand would shift to the right. These are just a few of the many possible ways the aggregate demand curve may shift. None of these explanations, however, has anything to do with changes in the price level.

Aggregate Supply Curve

The **aggregate supply curve** depicts the quantity of real GDP that is supplied by the economy at different price levels. The reasoning used to construct the aggregate supply curve differs from the reasoning used to construct the supply curves for individual goods and services. The supply curve for an individual good is drawn under the assumption that input prices remain constant. As the price of good X rises, sellers' per unit costs of providing good X do not change, and so sellers are willing to supply more of good X—hence, the upward slope of the supply curve for good X. The aggregate supply curve, however, is defined in terms of the *price level.* Increases in the price level will increase the price that producers can get for their products and thus induce more output. But an increase in the price will also have a second effect; it will eventually lead to increases in input prices as well, which, *ceteris paribus,* will cause producers to cut back. So, there is some uncertainty as to whether the economy will supply more real GDP as the price level rises. In order to address this issue, it has become customary to distinguish between two types of aggregate supply curves, the **short-run aggregate supply curve** and the **long-run aggregate supply curve.**

Short-run aggregate supply curve. The **short-run aggregate supply (SAS) curve** is considered a valid description of the supply schedule of the economy *only* in the short-run. The **short-run** is the period that begins immediately after an increase in the price level and that ends when *input prices* have increased in *the same proportion* to the increase in the price level.

Input prices are the prices paid to the providers of input goods and services. These input prices include the wages paid to workers, the interest paid to the providers of capital, the rent paid to landowners, and the prices paid to suppliers of intermediate goods. When the price level of final goods rises, the cost of living increases for those who provide input goods and services. Once these input providers realize that the cost of living has increased, they will increase the prices that they charge for their input goods and services in proportion to the increase in the price level for final goods.

The presumption underlying the *SAS* curve is that input providers *do not* or *cannot* take account of the increase in the general price level right away so that it takes some time—referred to as the short-run—for input prices to fully reflect changes in the price level for final goods. For example, workers often negotiate multi-year contracts with their employers. These contracts usually include a certain allowance for an increase in the price level, called a **cost of living adjustment (COLA).** The COLA, however, is based on expectations of the future price level that may turn out to be wrong. Suppose, for example, that workers *underestimate* the increase in the price level that occurs during the multi-year contract. Depending on the terms of the contract, the workers may not have the opportunity to correct their mistaken estimates of inflation until the contract expires. In this case, their wage increases will lag behind the increases in the price level for some time.

During the short-run, *sellers of final goods* are receiving higher prices for their products, without a proportional increase in the cost of their inputs. The higher the price level, the more these sellers will be willing to supply. The *SAS* curve—depicted in Figure 3-3(a)—is therefore upward sloping, reflecting the positive relationship that exists between the price level and the quantity of goods supplied in the short-run.

Figure 3-3 The aggregate supply curve

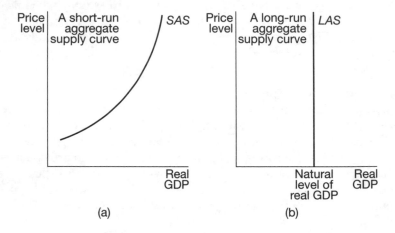

(a) (b)

Long-run aggregate supply curve. The **long-run aggregate supply (LAS) curve** describes the economy's supply schedule in the long-run. The **long-run** is defined as the period when input prices have completely adjusted to changes in the price level of final goods. In the long-run, the increase in prices that sellers receive for their final goods is completely offset by the proportional increase in the prices that sellers pay for inputs. The result is that the quantity of real GDP supplied by all sellers in the economy is independent of changes in the price level. The *LAS* curve— depicted in Figure 3-3(b)—is a vertical line, reflecting the fact that long-run aggregate supply is not affected by changes in the price level. Note that the *LAS* curve is vertical at the point labeled as the natural level of real GDP. The **natural level of real GDP** is defined as the level of real GDP that arises when the economy is *fully employing* all of its available input resources.

Changes in aggregate supply. Changes in aggregate supply are represented by shifts of the aggregate supply curve. An illustration of the ways in which the *SAS* and *LAS* curves can shift is provided in Figures 3-4(a) and 3-4(b). A shift to the *right* of the SAS curve from SAS_1 to SAS_2 or of the *LAS* curve from LAS_1 to LAS_2 means that at the same price levels the quantity supplied of real GDP has *increased*. A shift to the *left* of the *SAS* curve from SAS_1 to SAS_3 or of the *LAS* curve from LAS_1, to LAS_3 means that at the same price levels the quantity supplied of real GDP has *decreased*.

Figure 3-4   Shifts of the aggregate supply curve

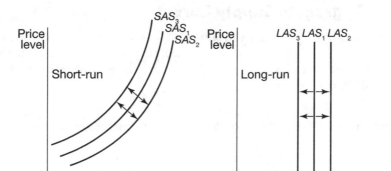

(a)   (b)

Like changes in aggregate demand, changes in aggregate supply are *not* caused by changes in the price level. Instead, they are primarily caused by changes in *two* other factors. The first of these is *a change in input prices.* For example, the price of oil, an input good, increased dramatically in the 1970s due to efforts by oil-exporting countries to restrict the quantity of oil sold. Many final goods and services use oil or oil products as inputs. Suppliers of these final goods and services faced rising costs and had to reduce their supply at all price levels. The *decrease* in aggregate supply, caused by the increase in input prices, is represented by a shift to the *left* of the *SAS* curve because the *SAS* curve is drawn under the assumption that input prices remain constant. An *increase* in aggregate supply due to a decrease in input prices is represented by a shift to the *right* of the *SAS* curve.

A second factor that causes the aggregate supply curve to shift is *economic growth. Positive* economic growth results from an increase in productive resources, such as labour and capital. With more resources, it is possible to produce more final goods and services, and hence, the natural level of real GDP increases. Positive economic growth is therefore represented by a shift to the *right* of the *LAS* curve. Similarly, *negative economic growth decreases* the natural level of real GDP, causing the *LAS* curve to shift to the left.

Combining the Aggregate Demand and Aggregate Supply Curves

When the aggregate demand and *SAS* curves are combined, as in Figure 3-5, the intersection of the two curves determines both the **equilibrium price level,** denoted by P^*, and the **equilibrium level of real GDP,** denoted by Y^*.

Figure 3-5 Equilibrium in the aggregate demand-aggregate supply model

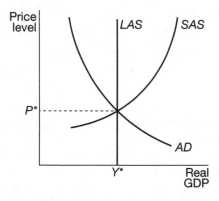

If it is further assumed that the economy is fully employing all of its resources, the equilibrium level of real GDP, Y^*, will correspond to the **natural level of real GDP,** and the *LAS* curve may be drawn as a vertical line at Y^*, as in Figure 3-5.

Consider what happens to this situation when the aggregate demand curve shifts to the *right* from AD_1 to AD_2, as in Figure 3-6.

The immediate, short-run effect is that the equilibrium price level increases from P_1 to P_2, and real GDP increases *above* its natural level, from Y_1 to Y_2. The increase in real GDP is due to the fact that input prices have not yet risen in response to the increase in the price level for final goods; the economy is still operating along the old *SAS* curve, SAS_1. Eventually, however, input providers will demand higher prices to reflect the increase in the general price level. Production costs will therefore increase, and the supply of real GDP will be reduced. This is represented by the shift to the *left* of the *SAS* curve from SAS_1 to SAS_2. The end result is a higher price level, P_3, at the same, natural level of real GDP, Y_1.

Figure 3-6   A change in the aggregate demand when the economy is at the natural level of real GDP

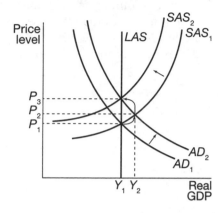

The graphical analysis presented in Figure 3-6 applies only to the case where there is zero economic growth, and the economy is already at the natural level of real GDP when aggregate demand increases. In the case where the economy is not fully employing all of its input resources and has therefore not yet attained its natural level of real GDP, an increase in aggregate demand—depicted in Figure 3-7 as a shift from AD_1, to AD_2— causes both an increase in the equilibrium price level from P_1 to P_2, and an increase in the equilibrium level of real GDP from Y_1 to Y_2.

Figure 3-7   A change in the aggregate demand when the economy is below the natural level of real GDP

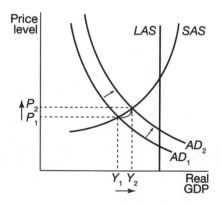

In this case, the increase in the equilibrium price level does not necessarily lead to an increase in input prices because the economy is not fully employing all of its input resources. When unemployed inputs are available, input prices do not tend to rise. The result, in this case, is that the *SAS* curve *does not* shift left and cancel out the increase in real GDP brought about by the increase in aggregate demand.

Chapter 4

CLASSICAL AND KEYNESIAN THEORIES OF OUTPUT AND EMPLOYMENT

The determination of equilibrium output, employment, and the price level in macroeconomics has been debated for many years. Two of the most widely discussed theories are the **classical** and **Keynesian theories.** The term *classical* is a reference to the economic theories of eighteenth- and nineteenth-century economists such as **Adam Smith, David Ricardo,** and **John Stuart Mill.** The term *Keynesian* is a reference to the economic theories of **John Maynard Keynes** and his followers. Keynesian economics has its origins in the Great Depression of the 1930s.

The Classical Theory

The fundamental principle of the **classical theory** is that the economy is self-regulating. Classical economists maintain that the economy is always capable of achieving the natural level of real GDP or output, which is the level of real GDP that is obtained when the economy's resources are *fully employed.* While circumstances arise from time to time that cause the economy to fall below or to exceed the natural level of real GDP, **self-adjustment mechanisms** exist within the market system that work to bring the economy back to the natural level of real GDP. The classical doctrine—that the economy is always at or near the natural level of real GDP—is based on two firmly held beliefs: **Say's Law** and the belief that prices, wages, and interest rates are flexible.

Say's Law. According to Say's Law, when an economy produces a certain level of real GDP, it also generates the income needed to purchase that level of real GDP. In other words, the economy is always capable of demanding all of the output that its workers and firms choose to produce. Hence, the economy is always capable of achieving the natural level of real GDP.

The achievement of the natural level of real GDP is not as simple as Say's Law would seem to suggest. While it is true that the income obtained from producing a certain level of real GDP must be sufficient to purchase that level of real GDP, there is no guarantee that all of this income will be spent. Some of this income will be *saved*. Income that is saved is not used to purchase consumption goods and services, implying that the demand for these goods and services will be *less* than the supply. If aggregate demand falls below aggregate supply due to aggregate saving, suppliers will cut back on their production and reduce the number of resources that they employ. When employment of the economy's resources falls below the full employment level, the equilibrium level of real GDP also falls below its natural level. Consequently, the economy may not achieve the natural level of real GDP if there is aggregate saving. The classical theorists' response is that the funds from aggregate saving are eventually borrowed and turned into investment expenditures, which *are* a component of real GDP. Hence, aggregate saving need not lead to a reduction in real GDP.

Consider, however, what happens when the funds from aggregate saving *exceed* the needs of all borrowers in the economy. In this situation, real GDP will fall below its natural level because investment expenditures will be less than the level of aggregate saving. This situation is illustrated in Figure 4-1.

Aggregate saving, represented by the curve S, is an upward-sloping function of the interest rate; as the interest rate rises, the economy tends to save more. Aggregate investment, represented by the curve I, is a downward-sloping function of the interest rate; as the interest rate rises, the cost of borrowing increases and investment expenditures decline. Initially, aggregate saving and investment are equivalent at the interest rate, i. If aggregate saving were to increase, causing the S curve to shift to the right to S', then at the same interest rate i, a **gap** emerges between investment and savings. Aggregate investment will be lower than aggregate saving, implying that equilibrium real GDP will be below its natural level.

Figure 4-1 Classical theory of interest rate adjustment in the money market

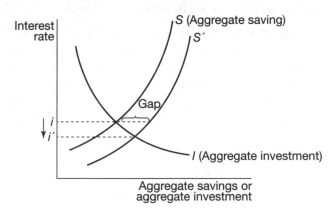

Flexible interest rates, wages, and prices. Classical economists believe that under these circumstances, the interest rate will *fall*, causing investors to demand more of the available savings. In fact, the interest rate will fall far enough—from i to i' in Figure 4-1—to make the supply of funds from aggregate saving equal to the demand for funds by all investors. Hence, an increase in savings will lead to an increase in investment expenditures through a reduction of the interest rate, and the economy will always return to the natural level of real GDP. The flexibility of the interest rate as well as other prices is the self-adjusting mechanism of the classical theory that ensures that real GDP is always at its natural level. The flexibility of the interest rate keeps the **money market,** or the **market for loanable funds,** in equilibrium all the time and thus prevents real GDP from falling below its natural level.

Similarly, flexibility of the wage rate keeps the labour market, or the market for workers, in equilibrium all the time. If the supply of workers exceeds firms' demand for workers, then wages paid to workers will fall so as to ensure that the work force is fully employed.

Classical economists believe that any unemployment that occurs in the labour market or in other resource markets should be considered **voluntary unemployment.** Voluntarily unemployed workers are unemployed because they refuse to accept lower wages. If they would only accept lower wages, firms would be eager to employ them.

Graphical illustration of the classical theory. Figure 3-6 illustrates the classical theory of output and price-level adjustment in response to an *increase* in aggregate demand. In Figure 3-6, the economy begins and ends up at the natural level of real GDP because the price level adjusts. The increase in aggregate demand was shown to cause an increase in the price level. Figure 4-2 considers the opposite case of a *decrease* in aggregate demand from AD_1 to AD_2.

Figure 4-2   Classical theory of output and price level adjustment during a recession

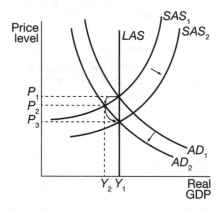

The immediate, short-run effect is that the economy moves down along the *SAS* curve labeled SAS_1, causing the equilibrium price level to fall from P_1 to P_2, and equilibrium real GDP to fall *below* its natural level of Y_1 to Y_2. If real GDP falls below its natural level, the economy's workers and resources arc not being fully employed. When there are unemployed resources, the classical theory predicts that the wages paid to these resources will fall. With the fall in wages, suppliers will be able to supply more goods at lower cost, causing the *SAS* curve to shift to the right from SAS_1 to SAS_2. The end result is that the equilibrium price level falls to P_3, but the economy returns to the natural level of real GDP. Figures 3-6 and 4-2 thus illustrate the notion of a self-regulating economy that is the hallmark of the classical theory.

The Keynesian Theory

Keynes's theory of the determination of equilibrium real GDP, employment, and prices focuses on the relationship between aggregate income and expenditure. Keynes used his **income-expenditure** model to argue that the economy's equilibrium level of output or real GDP may not correspond to the natural level of real GDP. In the income-expenditure model, the equilibrium level of real GDP is the level of real GDP that is consistent with the current level of aggregate expenditure. If the current level of aggregate expenditure is not sufficient to purchase all of the real GDP supplied, output will be cut back until the level of real GDP is equal to the level of aggregate expenditure. Hence, if the current level of aggregate expenditure is not sufficient to purchase the *natural* level of real GDP, then the equilibrium level of real GDP will lie somewhere *below* the natural level.

In this situation, the classical theorists believe that prices and wages will fall, reducing producer costs and increasing the supply of real GDP until it is again equal to the natural level of real GDP.

Sticky prices. Keynesians, however, believe that prices and wages are not so flexible. *They* believe that prices and wages are **sticky,** especially downward. The stickiness of prices and wages in the downward direction prevents the economy's resources from being fully employed and thereby prevents the economy from returning to the natural level of real GDP. Thus, the Keynesian theory is a rejection of Say's Law and the notion that the economy is self-regulating.

Keynes's income-expenditure model. Recall that real GDP can be decomposed into four component parts: aggregate expenditures on consumption, investment, government, and net exports. The **income-expenditure model** considers the relationship between these expenditures and current real national income. Aggregate expenditures on investment, *I*, government, *G*, and net exports, *NX*, are typically regarded as *autonomous* or *independent* of current income. The exception is aggregate expenditures on consumption. Keynes argues that *aggregate* consumption expenditures are determined primarily by current real national income. He suggests that aggregate consumption expenditures can be summarized by the equation

$$\text{aggregate consumption} = C + mpc(Y)$$

where *C* denotes autonomous consumption expenditure and *Y* is the level of current real income, which is equivalent to the value of current real

GDP. The **marginal propensity to consume** *(mpc)*, which multiplies *Y*, is the *fraction* of a change in real income that is currently consumed. In most economies, the *mpc* is quite high, ranging anywhere from .60 to .95. Note that as the level of *Y* increases, so too does the level of aggregate consumption.

Total **aggregate expenditure,** *AE,* can be written as the equation

$$AE = A + mpc(Y)$$

where *A* denotes total autonomous expenditure, or the sum $C + I + G + NX$. Different levels of autonomous expenditure, *A,* and real national income, *Y,* correspond to different levels of aggregate expenditure, *AE.*

Equilibrium real GDP in the income-expenditure model is found by setting current real national income, *Y,* equal to current aggregate expenditure, *AE.* Algebraically, the equilibrium condition that *Y = AE* implies that

$$Y = A + mpc(Y)$$
$$\rightarrow (1 - mpc)Y = A$$
$$\rightarrow \quad Y^* = m(A)$$

where
$$m = \frac{1}{(1 - mpc)}$$

In words, the equilibrium level of real GDP, *Y**, is equal to the level of autonomous expenditure, *A,* multiplied by *m,* the **Keynesian multiplier.** Because the *mpc* is the *fraction* of a change in real national income that is consumed, it always takes on values between 0 and 1. Consequently, the Keynesian multiplier, *m,* is always greater than 1, implying that equilibrium real GDP, *Y**, is always a *multiple* of autonomous aggregate expenditure, *A,* which explains why *m* is referred to as the Keynesian multiplier.

The determination of equilibrium real national income or GDP using the income-expenditure approach can be depicted graphically, as in Figure 4-3. This figure shows three different **aggregate expenditure curves,** labeled AE_1, AE_2, and AE_3, which correspond to three different levels of autonomous expenditure, A_1, A_2, and A_3. The upward slope of these *AE* curves is due to the positive value of the *mpc.* As real national income *Y* rises, so does the level of aggregate expenditure. The Keynesian condition for the determination of equilibrium real GDP is that *Y = AE.* This equilibrium condition is denoted in Figure 4-3 by the diagonal, 45° line, labeled *Y = AE.*

To find the level of equilibrium real national income or GDP, you simply find the intersection of the *AE curve* with the 45° line. The levels of real GDP that correspond to these intersection points are the *equilibrium* levels of real GDP, denoted in Figure 4-3 as Y_1, Y_2, and Y_3. Note that each *AE* curve corresponds to a different equilibrium *level* for Y. Note also that each Y is *a multiple* of the level of autonomous aggregate expenditure, *A*, as was found in the algebraic determination of the level of equilibrium real GDP.

Figure 4-3   The Keynesian income-expenditure approach to equilibrium real GDP

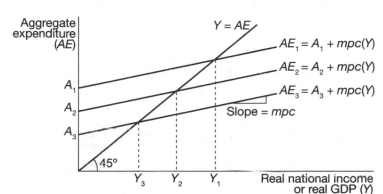

Graphical illustration of the Keynesian theory. The Keynesian theory of the determination of equilibrium output and prices makes use of both the income-expenditure model and the aggregate demand-aggregate supply model, as shown in Figure 4-4.

Suppose that the economy is initially at the natural *level* of real GDP that corresponds to Y_1 in Figure 4-4. Associated with this level of real GDP is an aggregate *expenditure* curve, AE_1. Now, suppose that autonomous expenditure declines, from A_1, to A_3, causing the *AE* curve to shift downward from AE_1 to AE_3. This decline in autonomous expenditure is also represented by a reduction in aggregate demand from AD_1 to AD_2. At the same price level, P_1, equilibrium real GDP has fallen from Y_1 to Y_3. However, the intersection of the *SAS* and AD_2 curves is at the lower price level, P_2, implying that the price level falls. The fall in the price level means that the aggregate expenditure curve will not fall all the way to AE_3 but will instead fall only to AE_2. Therefore, the new level of equilibrium real GDP is at Y_2, which lies below the natural level, Y_1.

Figure 4-4   The Keynesian income-expenditure approach and aggregate demand and supply

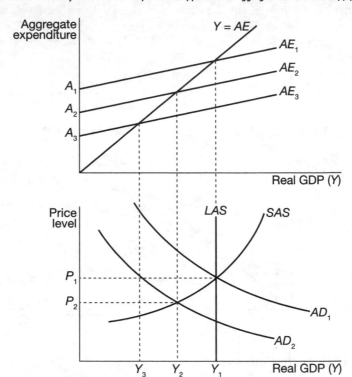

Keynes argues that prices will not fall further below P, because workers and other resources will resist any reduction in their wages, and this resistance will prevent suppliers from increasing their supplies. Hence, the *SAS* curve will not shift to the right as in the classical theory (compare with Figure 4-2) and the economy will remain at Y_2, where some of the economy's workers and resources are *unemployed*. Because these unemployed workers and resources earn no income, they cannot purchase goods and services. Consequently, the aggregate expenditure curve remains stuck at AE_2, preventing the economy from achieving the natural level of real GDP. Figure 4-4 therefore illustrates the Keynesians' rejection of Say's Law, price level flexibility, and the notion of a self-regulating economy.

Chapter 5

MONEY AND BANKING

The role of money and the banking system is an important part of the study of macroeconomics. Money, after all, is involved in nearly all economic transactions. This section explains the nature and functions of money, the demand and supply of money, and the role of the banking system in the money-creation process.

Definition of Money

What is **money?** Money is any good that is widely used and accepted in transactions involving the transfer of goods and services from one person to another. Economists differentiate among three different types of money: **commodity money, fiat money,** and **bank money.** Commodity money is a good whose value serves as the value of money. Gold coins are an example of commodity money. In most countries, commodity money has been replaced with fiat money. Fiat money is a good, the value of which is less than the value it represents as money. Dollar bills are an example of fiat money because their value as slips of printed paper is less than their value as money. Bank money consists of the **book credit** that banks extend to their depositors. Transactions made using **cheques** drawn on deposits held at banks involve the use of bank money.

Functions of Money

Money is often defined in terms of the three **functions** or **services** that it provides. Money serves as a **medium of exchange,** as a **store of value,** and as a **unit of account.**

Medium of exchange. Money's most important function is as a medium of exchange to facilitate transactions. Without money, all transactions would have to be conducted by **barter,** which involves direct exchange of one good or service for another. The difficulty with a **barter system** is that in order to obtain a particular good or service from a supplier, one has to possess a good or service of equal value, which the supplier also desires. In other words, in a barter system, exchange can take place *only* if there is a **double coincidence of wants** between two transacting parties. The likelihood of a double coincidence of wants, however, is small and makes the exchange of goods and services rather difficult. Money effectively eliminates the double coincidence of wants problem by serving as a medium of exchange that is accepted in all transactions, by all parties, regardless of whether they desire each others' goods and services.

Store of value. In order to be a medium of exchange, money must hold its value over time; that is, it must be a store of value. If money could not be stored for some period of time and still remain valuable in exchange, it would not solve the double coincidence of wants problem and therefore would not be adopted as a medium of exchange. As a store of value, money is not unique; many other stores of value exist, such as land, works of art, and even baseball cards and stamps. Money may not even be the best store of value because it depreciates with inflation. However, money is more **liquid** than most other stores of value because as a medium of exchange, it is readily accepted everywhere. Furthermore, money is an easily transported store of value that is available in a number of convenient denominations.

Unit of account. Money also functions as a unit of account, providing a *common measure of the value* of goods and services being exchanged. Knowing the value or price of a good, in terms of money, enables both the supplier and the purchaser of the good to make decisions about how much of the good to supply and how much of the good to purchase.

The Demand for Money

The demand for money is affected by several factors, including the level of income, interest rates, and inflation as well as uncertainty about the future. The way in which these factors affect money demand is usually explained in terms of the three motives for demanding money: the **transactions,** the **precautionary,** and the **speculative motives.**

Transactions motive. The **transactions motive** for demanding money arises from the fact that most transactions involve an exchange of money. Because it is necessary to have money available for transactions, money will be demanded. The total number of transactions made in an economy tends to increase over time as income rises. Hence, as income or GDP rises, the **transactions demand** for money also rises.

Precautionary motive. People often demand money as *a precaution* against an uncertain future. Unexpected expenses, such as medical or car repair bills, often require *immediate payment.* The need to have money available in such situations is referred to as the precautionary motive for demanding money.

Speculative motive. Money, like other stores of value, is an **asset.** The demand for an asset depends on both its **rate of return** and its **opportunity cost.** Typically, money holdings provide *no* rate of return and often depreciate in value due to inflation. The opportunity cost of holding money is the interest rate that can be earned by lending or investing one's money holdings. The **speculative motive** for demanding money arises in situations where holding money is perceived to be *less risky* than the alternative of lending the money or investing it in some other asset

For example, if a stock market crash seemed imminent, the speculative motive for demanding money would come into play; those expecting the market to crash would sell their stocks and hold the proceeds as money. The presence of a speculative motive for demanding money is also affected by *expectations of future interest rates and inflation.* If interest rates are expected to rise, the opportunity cost of holding money will become greater, which in turn diminishes the speculative motive for demanding money. Similarly, expectations of higher inflation presage a greater depreciation in the purchasing power of money and therefore lessen the speculative motive for demanding money.

Supply of Money

There are several definitions of the **supply of money.** *M*1 is narrowest and most commonly used. It includes all **currency** (notes and coins) in circulation, all **chequeable deposits** held at banks (bank money), and all **traveler's cheques.** A somewhat broader measure of the supply of money is *M*2, which includes all of *M*1 plus **savings** and **time deposits** held at banks. An even broader measure of the money supply is *M*3, which includes all of *M*2 plus large denomination, long-term time deposits—for example, **certificates of deposit** (CDs) in amounts over $100,000. Most discussions of the money supply, however, are in terms of the *M*1 definition of the money supply.

Banking business. In order to understand the factors that determine the supply of money, one must first understand the role of the **banking** sector in the money-creation process. Banks perform two crucial functions. First, they receive funds from depositors and, in return, provide these depositors with a checkable source of funds or with interest payments. Second, they use the funds that they receive from depositors to make loans to borrowers; that is, they serve as **intermediaries** in the borrowing and lending process.

When banks receive deposits, they do not keep *all* of these deposits on hand because they know that depositors will not demand all of these deposits at once. Instead, banks keep only a *fraction* of the deposits that they receive. The deposits that banks keep on hand are known as the banks' **reserves.** When depositors withdraw deposits, they are paid out of the banks' reserves. The **reserve requirement** is the *fraction* of deposits set aside for withdrawal purposes. The reserve requirement is determined by the nation's banking authority, a government agency known as the **central bank.** Deposits that banks are not required to set aside as reserves can be lent to borrowers, in the form of **loans.** Banks earn **profits** by borrowing funds from depositors at zero or low rates of interest and using these funds to make loans at higher rates of interest.

A **balance sheet** for a typical bank is given in Table 5-1. The balance sheet summarizes the bank's **assets** and **liabilities.** Assets are valuable items that the bank owns and consist primarily of the bank's reserves and loans. Liabilities are valuable items that the bank owes to others and consist primarily of the bank's **deposit** liabilities to its depositors. In Table 5-1, the bank's assets (reserves and loans) total $1 million. The bank's liabilities (deposits) total $1 million. A banking firm's assets must always equal its liabilities.

Table 5-1   The Balance Sheet of a Typical Bank

Assets		Liabilities	
Reserves	$100,000	Deposits	$1,000,000
Loans	900,000		

You can infer from Table 5-1 that the **reserve requirement** in this example is 10%.

How banks create money. Consider what happens when the same bank receives a $100,000 deposit from one of its depositors. The bank is required to set aside 10% of this deposit, or $10,000, as reserves. It then lends out its **excess reserves**—in this case, the remaining $90,000 of the initial deposit. Suppose, for the sake of simplicity, that all borrowers redeposit their loans into the same bank. The bank thus receives $90,000 in new deposits of which it sets $9,000 aside as reserves and lends out all of its excess reserves. Suppose again that all borrowers redeposit their loans in the same bank, that the hank sets aside a portion of these deposits, and that the bank then lends out the remainder, which is again redeposited in the bank and so on and so on. This repeated chain of events is summarized in Table 5-2.

Table 5-2   Multiple Expansion of Deposits

Round	New deposits	New reserves	New loans
1	$100,000	$10,000	$90,000
2	90,000	9,000	81,000
3	81,000	8,100	72,900
4	72,900	7,290	65,610
5	65,610	6,561	59,049
.	.	.	.
.	.	.	.
.	+.	+.	+.
	$1,000,000	$100,000	$900,000

If one were to follow this **multiple deposit expansion** process to its completion, the end result would be that the bank's deposits would increase by $1 million, its loans would increase by $900,000, and its reserves would increase by $100,000, all due to the initial deposit of $100,000.

Money multiplier. The amount by which bank deposits expand in response to an increase in **excess reserves** is found through the use of the **money multiplier,** which is given by the formula

$$\text{money multiplier} = \frac{1}{\text{reserve requirement}}$$

In the example of deposit expansion found in Table 5-2, the reserve requirement is 10%, so the money multiplier in this case is $(1/10) = 10$. The excess reserves resulting from the initial deposit of $100,000 are $90,000. Multiplying $90,000 by the money multiplier, 10, yields $900,000, which is the amount of *additional* deposits created by the banking system as the result of the initial $100,000 deposit.

In reality, loan recipients do not deposit all of their loan funds into a bank. More typically, they hold a fraction of their loan funds as currency. If some loan funds are held as currency, then there is a leakage of money out of the banking system. In this case, the money multiplier will still be greater than 1, but it will be *less* than the inverse of the reserve requirement.

Central banking and the supply of money. A portion of each nation's money supply ($M1$) is controlled by a government agency known as the **central bank.** The central bank is unique in that it is the only bank that can issue currency. The U.S. central bank is called the **Federal Reserve Bank** but is frequently referred to as "the Fed." The Fed issues all U.S. dollar bills, known as Federal Reserve Notes. Thus, the Fed has control over the supply of the U.S. **currency.** The Fed also has control over the private **bank reserves** that banks entrust to the Fed. Banks hold a portion of their required reserves with the Fed because the Fed acts as a **clearing house** for all sorts of transactions between banks—for example, the processing of all cheques.

The Fed's *liabilities* therefore consist of all Federal Reserve Notes in circulation plus all private bank deposits held at the Fed as reserves. On the *asset* side, the Fed owns a large amount of government debt in the form of U.S. **government bonds.** These bonds have been issued by the U.S. Treasury to pay for current and past government deficits. A simplified example of the Fed's balance sheet is provided in Table 5-3. Note that the Fed's total liabilities are equal to its total assets.

Table 5-3   The Balance Sheet of the Fed ($ values are in millions)

Assets	Liabilities
Government bonds $300	Federal Reserve notes $250
	Reserves of private banks 50

The Fed's control over the money supply stems from its ability to change the composition of its balance sheet. For example, the Fed may decide to purchase additional government bonds on the open market from bondholders or private banks. This type of action is referred to as an **open market operation** by the Fed. In exchange for these government bonds, the Fed increases the reserves of private banks by the amount of the purchase. Banks, in turn, lend out their excess reserves and initiate the multiple deposit expansion process discussed above. Thus, when the Fed *buys* U.S. government bonds on the open market, it increases the supply of money by increasing bank reserves and inducing an expansion in the amount of deposits. Similarly, when the Fed *sells* some of its stock of U.S. government bonds to bondholders or private banks, the Fed compensates itself for the sale by reducing the reserves of private banks. The *sale* of government bonds by the Fed *reduces* the supply of money by reducing the reserves available to private banks and thereby decreasing the amount of deposit expansion that is possible.

The Fed can also control the supply of money by its choice of the **reserve requirement.** Recall that the money multiplier is the reciprocal of the reserve requirement. If the Fed *increases* the reserve requirement, the money multiplier *decreases,* implying that deposit creation and the money supply are *reduced.* If the Fed *decreases* the reserve requirement, the money multiplier *increases*, causing both the creation of deposits and the money supply to expand further.

Chapter 6

FISCAL AND MONETARY POLICY

Government economic policies designed to influence macroeconomic performance are of two types: **fiscal policy** and **monetary policy.** Fiscal policy involves the use of government expenditures and taxation, while monetary policy is concerned with control of the money supply and credit market conditions. The goal of both types of government policies, however, is the same, namely to promote price level stability, full employment, and the achievement of the natural level of real GDP.

Fiscal Policy

Fiscal policy is carried out by the legislative and/or the executive branches of government. The two main **instruments** of fiscal policy are **government expenditures** and **taxes.** The government collects taxes in order to finance expenditures on a number of **public goods and services**—for example, highways and national defense.

Budget deficits and surpluses. When government expenditures *exceed* government tax revenues in a given year, the government is running a budget deficit for that year. The *budget deficit*, which is the difference between government expenditures and tax revenues, is financed by government borrowing; the government issues long-term, interest-bearing bonds and uses the proceeds to finance the deficit. The total stock of government bonds and interest payments outstanding, from both the present and the past, is known as the **national debt.** Thus, when the government finances a deficit by borrowing, it is *adding* to the national debt. When government expenditures are *less* than tax revenues in a given year, the government is running a budget surplus for that year. The **budget surplus** is the difference between tax revenues and government expenditures. The revenues from the budget surplus are typically used to *reduce* any existing national debt. In the case where government expenditures are exactly equal to tax revenues in a given year, the government is running a **balanced budget** for that year.

Expansionary and contractionary fiscal policy. Expansionary fiscal policy is defined as an *increase* in government expenditures and/or a *decrease* in taxes that causes the government's budget deficit to increase or its budget surplus to decrease. **Contractionary fiscal policy** is defined as a *decrease* in government expenditures and/or an *increase* in taxes that causes the government's budget deficit to decrease or its budget surplus to increase.

Classical and Keynesian views of fiscal policy. The belief that expansionary and contractionary fiscal policies can be used to influence macroeconomic performance is most closely associated with Keynes and his followers. The classical view of expansionary or contractionary fiscal policies is that such policies are unnecessary because there are market mechanisms—for example, the flexible adjustment of prices and wages—which serve to keep the economy at or near the natural level of real GDP at all times. Accordingly, classical economists believe that the government should run a balanced budget each and every year.

Combating a recession using expansionary fiscal policy. Keynesian theories of output and employment were developed in the midst of the Great Depression of the 1930s, when unemployment rates in Canada, the U.S., and Europe exceeded 25% and the growth rate of real GDP declined steadily for most of the decade. Keynes and his followers believed that the way to combat the prevailing recessionary climate was not to wait for prices and wages to adjust but to engage in expansionary fiscal policy instead. The Keynesians' argument in favour of expansionary fiscal policy is illustrated in Figure 6-1.

Figure 6-1　Combating a recession using expansionary fiscal policy

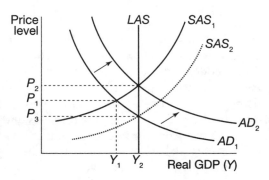

Assume that the economy is initially in a recession. The equilibrium level of real GDP, Y_1, lies below the natural level, Y_2, implying that there is less than full employment of the economy's resources. Classical economists believe that the presence of unemployed resources causes wages to fall, reducing costs to suppliers and causing the SAS curve to shift from SAS_1 to SAS_2 thereby restoring the economy to full employment. Keynesians, however, argue that wages are sticky downward and will not adjust quickly enough to reflect the reality of unemployed resources.

Consequently, the recessionary climate may persist for a long time. The way out of this difficulty, according to the Keynesians, is to run a budget deficit by increasing government expenditures in excess of current tax receipts. The increase in government expenditures should be sufficient to cause the aggregate demand curve to shift to the right from AD_1 to AD_2, restoring the economy to the natural level of real GDP. This increase in government expenditures need not, of course, be equal to the difference between Y_1 and Y_2. Recall that any increase in autonomous aggregate expenditures, including government expenditures, has *a multiplier* effect on aggregate demand. Hence, the government needs only to increase its expenditures by a small amount to cause aggregate demand to increase by the amount necessary to achieve the natural level of real GDP.

Keynesians argue that expansionary fiscal policy provides a quick way out of a recession and is to be preferred to waiting for wages and prices to adjust, which can take a long time. As Keynes once said, "In the long run, we are all dead."

Combating inflation using contractionary fiscal policy. Keynesians also argue that fiscal policy can be used to combat expected increases in the rate of inflation. Suppose that the economy is already at the natural level of real GDP and that aggregate demand is projected to increase further, which will cause the AD curve in Figure 6-2 to shift from AD_1 to AD_2.

Figure 6-2 Combating inflation using contractionary fiscal policy

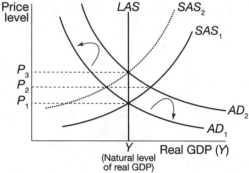

As real GDP rises above its natural level, prices also rise, prompting an increase in wages and other resource prices and causing the *SAS* curve to shift from SAS_1 to SAS_2. The end result is inflation of the price level from P_1 to P_3, with no change in real GDP. The government can head off this inflation by engaging in a **contractionary** fiscal policy designed to reduce aggregate demand by enough to prevent the *AD* curve from shifting out to AD_2. Again, the government needs only to decrease expenditures or increase taxes by a small amount because of the multiplier effects that such actions will have.

Secondary effects of fiscal policy. Classical economists point out that the Keynesian view of the effectiveness of fiscal policy tends to ignore the **secondary effects** that fiscal policy can have on credit market conditions. When the government pursues an expansionary fiscal policy, it finances its deficit spending by borrowing funds from the nation's credit market. Assuming that the money supply remains constant, the government's borrowing of funds in the credit market tends to reduce the amount of funds available and thereby drives up interest rates. Higher interest rates, in turn, tend to reduce or "crowd out" aggregate investment expenditures and consumer expenditures that are sensitive to interest rates. Hence, the effectiveness of expansionary fiscal policy in stimulating aggregate demand will be mitigated to some degree by this **crowding-out effect.**

The same holds true for contractionary fiscal policies designed to combat expected inflation. If the government reduces its expenditures and thereby reduces its borrowing, the supply of available funds in the credit market increases, causing the interest rate to fall. Aggregate demand increases as the private sector increases its investment and interest-sensitive consumption expenditures. Hence, contractionary fiscal policy leads to a **crowding-in effect** on the part of the private sector. This crowding-in effect mitigates the effectiveness of the contractionary fiscal policy in counteracting rising aggregate demand and inflationary pressures.

Monetary Policy

Monetary policy is conducted by a nation's central bank. In the U.S., monetary policy is carried out by the Fed. The Fed has three main instruments that it uses to conduct monetary policy: **open market operations, changes in reserve requirements,** and **changes in the discount rate.** Recall from the earlier discussion of money and banking that open market operations involve Fed purchases and sales of U.S. government bonds. When the Fed *purchases* government bonds, it increases the reserves of the banking sector, and by the multiple deposit expansion process, the supply of money *increases.* When the Fed sells some of its stock of U.S. government bonds, the end result is a *decrease* in the supply of money. If the Fed *increases* bank reserve requirements, the banking sector's excess reserves are reduced, leading to a *reduction* in the supply of money; *a decrease* in reserve requirements induces an *increase* in the supply of money.

The **discount rate** is the interest rate the Fed charges banks that need to borrow reserves in order to meet reserve requirements. From time to time, unanticipated withdrawals leave banks with insufficient reserves. Banks can make up for deficiencies in their required reserves by borrowing from the Fed at the discount rate. If the Fed sets the discount rate *high* relative to market interest rates, it becomes more costly for banks to fall below reserve requirements. Accordingly, banks will hold more excess reserves, which tends to reduce the multiple expansion of deposits and the supply of money. Similarly, when the discount rate is *low* relative to market interest rates, banks tend to hold fewer excess reserves, allowing for greater deposit expansion and an *increase* in the supply of money.

Expansionary and contractionary monetary policy. The Fed is engaging in **expansionary monetary policy** when it uses any of its instruments of monetary policy in such a way as to cause an increase in the supply of money. The Fed is said to engage in **contractionary monetary policy** when it uses its instruments to effect a reduction in the supply of money.

Classical view of monetary policy. The classical economists' view of monetary policy is based on the **quantity theory of money.** According to this theory, an increase (decrease) in the quantity of money leads to a proportional increase (decrease) in the price level. The quantity theory of money is usually discussed in terms of the **equation of exchange,** which is given by the expression

$$MV = PY$$

In this expression, P denotes the price level, and Y denotes the level of current real GDP. Hence, PY represents current **nominal GDP;** M denotes the supply of money over which the Fed has some control; and V denotes the **velocity of circulation,** which is the average number of times a dollar is spent on final goods and services over the course of a year. The equation of exchange is an **identity** which states that the current market value of all final goods and services—nominal GDP—must equal the supply of money multiplied by the average number of times a dollar is used in transactions in a given year. The quantity theory of money requires *two assumptions,* which transform the equation of exchange from an identity to a theory of money and monetary policy.

Recall that the classical economists believe that the economy is always at or near the natural level of real GDP. Accordingly, classical economists assume that Y in the equation of exchange is fixed, at least in the short-run. Furthermore, classical economists argue that the velocity of circulation of money tends to remain constant so that V can also be regarded as fixed. *Assuming that both Y and V are fixed,* it follows that if the Fed were to engage in expansionary (or contractionary) monetary policy, leading to an increase (or decrease) in M, the only effect would be to increase (or decrease) the price level, P, in direct proportion to the change in M. In other words, expansionary monetary policy can only lead to *inflation,* and contractionary monetary policy can only lead to *deflation* of the price level.

Keynesian view of monetary policy. Keynesians do not believe in the *direct* link between the supply of money and the price level that emerges from the classical quantity theory of money. They reject the notion that the economy is always at or near the natural level of real GDP so that Y in the equation of exchange can be regarded as fixed. They also reject the proposition that the velocity of circulation of money is constant and can cite evidence to support their case.

Keynesians do believe in an *indirect* link between the money supply and real GDP. They believe that expansionary monetary policy increases the supply of loanable funds available through the banking system, causing interest rates to fall. With lower interest rates, aggregate expenditures on investment and interest-sensitive consumption goods usually *increase,* causing real GDP to rise. Hence, monetary policy can affect real GDP indirectly.

Keynesians, however, remain skeptical about the effectiveness of monetary policy. They point out that expansionary monetary policies that increase the reserves of the banking system need not lead to a multiple expansion of the money supply because banks can simply refuse to lend out their excess reserves. Furthermore, the lower interest rates that result from an expansionary monetary policy *need not* induce an increase in aggregate investment and consumption expenditures because firms' and households' demands for investment and consumption goods may not be sensitive to the lower interest rates. For these reasons, Keynesians tend to place less emphasis on the effectiveness of *monetary* policy and more emphasis on the effectiveness of fiscal policy, which they regard as having a more direct effect on real GDP.

Monetarist view of monetary policy. Since the 1950s, a new view of monetary policy, called **monetarism,** has emerged that disputes the Keynesian view that monetary policy is relatively ineffective. Adherents of monetarism, called **monetarists,** argue that the *demand* for money is stable and is not very sensitive to changes in the rate of interest. Hence, expansionary monetary policies only serve to create a surplus of money that households will quickly spend, thereby increasing aggregate demand. Unlike classical economists, monetarists acknowledge that the economy may not always be operating at the full employment level of real GDP. Thus, in the short-run, monetarists argue that expansionary monetary policies may increase the level of real GDP by increasing aggregate demand. However, in the long-run, when the economy is operating at the full employment level, monetarists argue that the classical quantity theory remains a good approximation of the link between the supply of money, the price level, and the real GDP—that is, in the long-run, expansionary monetary policies only lead to inflation and do not affect the level of real GDP.

Monetarists are particularly concerned with the potential for abuse of monetary policy and destabilization of the price level. They often cite the contractionary monetary policies of the Fed during the Great Depression, policies that they blame for the tremendous deflation of that period. Monetarists believe that **persistent inflations** (or **deflations**) are purely monetary phenomena brought about by persistent expansionary (or contractionary) monetary policies. As a means of combating persistent periods of inflation or deflation, monetarists argue in favour of a **fixed money supply rule.** They believe that the Fed should conduct monetary policy so as to keep the growth rate of the money supply fixed at a rate that is equal to the real growth rate of the economy over time. Thus, monetarists believe that monetary policy should serve to accommodate increases in real GDP without causing either inflation or deflation.

MICROECONOMICS

Chapter 7
THEORY OF THE CONSUMER

The branch of economics known as **microeconomics** focuses on the behaviour of **individual consumers** and **individual firms.** This section reviews the **theory of the consumer,** and the following sections review the **theory of the firm.** The theory of the consumer describes how individual consumers make economic choices, given their **preferences,** their **incomes,** and the **prices** of the goods and services that they desire to purchase.

Utility and Preferences

Individuals consume goods and services because they derive pleasure or satisfaction from doing so. Economists use the term *utility* to describe the pleasure or satisfaction that a consumer obtains from his or her consumption of goods and services. Utility is a subjective measure of pleasure or satisfaction that varies from individual to individual according to each individual's **preferences.** For example, if an individual's choices for a Saturday evening are to watch television, go out to dinner, or go to a movie, then, depending on that individual's preferences, he or she will attribute different levels of utility to each of these three activities. Of course, it is not possible to measure utility, nor is it possible to claim that one individual's utility is higher than another's. Utility is just a unitless measure that economists have found useful in their explanation of consumer choice.

Total and marginal utility. The utility that an individual receives from consuming a certain amount of a particular good or service is referred to as that individual's **total utility.** The **marginal utility** of a good or service is the *addition* to total utility that an individual receives from consuming *one more unit* of that good or service.

Law of diminishing marginal utility. The **law of diminishing marginal utility** states that the marginal utility that one receives from consuming successive units of the same good or service will eventually *decrease* as the number of units consumed *increases*. As an example of the law of diminishing marginal utility, consider the utility that one obtains from drinking successive glasses of lemonade on a hot day. Suppose the first glass just begins to quench one's thirst. After two glasses, however, the thirst has all but disappeared. A third glass of lemonade might also provide some utility, but not as much as the second glass. A fourth glass cannot be finished. In this example, the marginal utility—the addition to total utility that one obtains from drinking lemonade on a hot day—is increasing for the first two glasses but is decreasing beginning with the third glass and would continue to decrease if one were to consume further glasses.

Consumer Equilibrium

When consumers make choices about the quantity of goods and services to consume, it is presumed that their objective is to **maximize total utility.** In maximizing total utility, the consumer faces a number of **constraints,** the most important of which are the consumer's *income* and the *prices* of the goods and services that the consumer wishes to consume. The consumer's effort to maximize total utility, subject to these constraints, is referred to as the **consumer's problem.** The solution to the consumer's problem, which entails decisions about how much the consumer will consume of a number of goods and services, is referred to as **consumer equilibrium.**

Determination of consumer equilibrium. Consider the simple case of a consumer who cares about consuming only two goods: good 1 and good 2. This consumer knows the prices of goods 1 and 2 and has a fixed income or budget that can be used to purchase quantities of goods 1 and 2. The consumer will purchase quantities of goods 1 and 2 so as to completely exhaust the budget for such purchases. The actual quantities purchased of each good are determined by the condition for consumer equilibrium, which is

$$\frac{\text{marginal utility of good 1}}{\text{price of good 1}} = \frac{\text{marginal utility of good 2}}{\text{price of good 2}}$$

This condition states that the marginal utility per dollar spent on good 1 must equal the marginal utility per dollar spent on good 2. If, for example, the marginal utility per dollar spent on good 1 were higher than the marginal utility per dollar spent on good 2, then it would make sense for the consumer to purchase more of good 1 rather than purchasing any more of good 2. After purchasing more and more of good 1, the marginal utility of good 1 will eventually fall due to the law of diminishing marginal utility, so that the marginal utility per dollar spent on good 1 will eventually equal that of good 2. Of course, the amount purchased of goods 1 and 2 cannot be limitless and will depend not only on the marginal utilities per dollar spent, but also on the consumer's budget.

An example. To illustrate how the consumer equilibrium condition determines the *quantity* of goods 1 and 2 that the consumer demands, suppose that the price of good 1 is $2 per unit and the price of good 2 is $1 per unit. Suppose also that the consumer has a budget of $5. The marginal utility *(MU)* that the consumer receives from consuming 1 to 4 units of goods 1 and 2 is reported in Table 7-1. Here, marginal utility is measured in fictional units called *utils,* which serve to quantify the consumer's additional utility or satisfaction from consuming different quantities of goods 1 and 2. The larger the number of utils, the greater is the consumer's marginal utility from consuming that unit of the good. Table 7-1 also reports the ratio of the consumer's marginal utility to the price of each good. For example, the consumer receives 24 utils from consuming the first unit of good 1, and the price of good 1 is $2. Hence, the ratio of the marginal utility of the first unit of good 1 to the price of good 1 is 12.

Table 7-1   Illustration of Consumer Equilibrium
Price of good 1 = $2, Price of good 2 = $1, Budget = $5

Units of good 1	MU of good 1	MU/price of good 1	Units of good 2	MU of good 2	MU/price of good 2
1	24	12	1	9	9
2	18	9	2	8	8
3	12	6	3	5	5
4	6	3	4	1	1

The consumer equilibrium is found by comparing the marginal utility per dollar spent (the ratio of the marginal utility to the price of a good) for goods 1 and 2, subject to the constraint that the consumer does not exceed her budget of $5. The marginal utility per dollar spent on the first unit of good 1 is greater than the marginal utility per dollar spent on the first unit of good 2 (12 utils > 9 utils). Because the price of good 1 is $2 per unit, the consumer can afford to purchase this first unit of good 1, and so she does. She now has $5 – $2 = $3 remaining in her budget. The consumer's next step is to compare the marginal utility per dollar spent on the *second* unit of good 1 with marginal utility per dollar spend on the *first* unit of good 2. Because these ratios are both equal to 9 utils, the consumer is *indifferent* between purchasing the second unit of good 1 and first unit of good 2, so she purchases both. She can afford to do so because the second unit of good 1 costs $2 and the first unit of good 2 costs $1, for a total of $3. At this point, the consumer has exhausted her budget of $5 and has arrived at the consumer equilibrium, where the marginal utilities per dollar spent are equal. The consumer's equilibrium choice is to purchase 2 units of good 1 and 1 unit of good 2.

The condition for consumer equilibrium can be extended to the more realistic case where the consumer must choose how much to consume of many different goods. When there are $N > 2$ goods to choose from, the consumer equilibrium condition is to equate all of the marginal utilities per dollar spent,

$$\frac{\text{marginal utility of good 1}}{\text{price of good 1}} = \frac{\text{marginal utility of good 2}}{\text{price of good 2}} = \cdots = \frac{\text{marginal utility of good } N}{\text{price of good } N}$$

subject to the constraint that the consumer's purchases do not exceed her budget.

Consumer Equilibrium and Changes in Prices

The consumer's choice of how much to consume of various goods depends on the prices of those goods. If prices change, the consumer's equilibrium choice will also change. To see how, consider again the example considered above where the consumer must decide how much to consume of goods 1 and 2. Suppose that the price of good 1 *increases* from $2 per unit to $3 per unit, while the price of good 2 remains unchanged at $1 per unit Everything else remains the same; the consumer's budget is still $5, and the marginal utility that the consumer receives from each additional unit of goods 1 and 2 is unchanged.

However, the ratio of the marginal utility of good 1 to the price of good 1 is now changed, due to the increase in the price of good 1. The new situation is reported in Table 7-2.

The increase in the price of good 1 to $3 lowers the marginal utility per dollar spent on good 1 relative to the case where the price of good 1 was $2. The new consumer equilibrium is found as before, by comparing the marginal utility per dollar spent on good 1 with the marginal utility per dollar spent on good 2. The consumer's new equilibrium choice is to consume 1 unit of good 1 and 2 units of good 2 because these quantities have the same marginal utility per dollar spent, and the purchase of these quantities completely exhausts the consumer's budget of $5.

Table 7-2   Illustration of Consumer Equilibrium
Price of good 1 = $3, Price of good 2 = $1, Budget = $5

Units of good 1	MU of good 1	MU/price of good 1	Units of good 2	MU of good 2	MU/price of good 2
1	24	8	1	9	9
2	18	6	2	8	8
3	12	4	3	5	5
4	6	2	4	1	1

The effect of a price change on the consumer's equilibrium choice is often divided into *two* effects—known at the substitution effect of a price change and the income effect of a price change.

Substitution effect of a price change. When the price of a good changes, the price of that good relative to the price of other goods also changes. *Relative* price changes cause consumers to substitute from one good to another—this is known as the **substitution effect.** The substitution effect is illustrated in the example considered above. As the price of good 1 rises from $2 to $3, good 1 becomes more expensive relative to good 2, and good 2 becomes less expensive relative to good 1. The consumer's response to the price increase is to substitute her consumption away from good 1 and toward good 2; she changes her consumption choice from 2 units of good 1 and 1 unit of good 2 to 1 unit of good 1 and 2 units of good 2.

Income effect of a price change. The **income effect** takes account of how price changes affect consumption choices by changing the real purchasing power or real income of the consumer. In the example above, the increase in the price of good 1 from $2 to $3 reduces the consumer's real purchasing power. Prior to the price change, the consumer was able to purchase 2 units of good 1 and 1 unit of good 2 using her budget of $5. After the price of good 1 rises to $3, the consumer is no longer able to purchase this same bundle of goods because it would cost $7 and she has only $5. Accordingly, she must reduce her expenditures. The portion of her change in the consumption of good 1 that is attributable to the change in her real purchasing power or real income is the *income effect* of the price change.

Individual Demand and Market Demand

The consumer equilibrium condition determines the quantity of each good the individual consumer will demand. As the example above illustrates, the individual consumer's demand for a particular good—call it good X—will satisfy the law of demand and can therefore be depicted by a downward-sloping **individual demand curve.** The individual consumer, however, is only one of many participants in the market for good X. The **market demand curve** for good X includes the quantities of good X demanded by *all* participants in the market for good X. The market demand curve is found by taking the **horizontal summation** of all individual demand curves. For example, suppose that there were just two consumers in the market for good X, Consumer 1 and Consumer 2. These two consumers have different individual demand curves corresponding to their different preferences for good X. The two individual demand curves are depicted in Figure 7-1, along with the market demand curve for good X.

Figure 7-1 Derivation of the market demand curve from consumers' individual demand curves

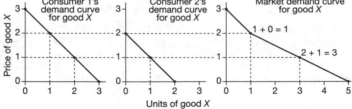

The market demand curve for good *X* is found by summing together the quantities that both consumers demand at each price. For example, at a price of $1, Consumer 1 demands 2 units while Consumer 2 demands 1 unit; so, the market demand is 2 + 1 = 3 units of good *X*. In more general settings, where there are more than two consumers in the market for some good, the same principle continues to apply; the market demand curve would be the horizontal summation of all the market participants' individual demand curves.

Consumer Surplus

The difference between the maximum price that consumers are willing to pay for a good and the market price that they actually pay for a good is referred to as the **consumer surplus.** The determination of consumer surplus is illustrated in Figure 7-2, which depicts the market demand curve for some good.

The market price is $5, and the equilibrium quantity demanded is 5 units of the good. The market demand curve reveals that consumers are willing to pay at least $9 for the first unit of the good, $8 for the second unit, $7 for the third unit, and $6 for the fourth unit.

Figure 7-2   Calculation of consumer surplus

However, they can purchase 5 units of the good for just $5 per unit. Their surplus from the first unit purchased is therefore $9 − $5 = $4. Similarly, their surpluses from the second, third, and fourth units purchased are $3, $2, and $1, respectively. These surpluses are illustrated by the vertical bars drawn in Figure 7-2. The sum total of these surpluses is the *consumer surplus*:

$$\$4 + \$3 + \$2 + \$1 = \$10$$

The value $10, however, is only a crude approximation of the true consumer surplus in this example. The *true* consumer surplus is given by the area below the market demand curve and above the market price. This area consists of a triangle with base of length 5 and height of length 5. Applying the rule for the area of a triangle—one half the base multiplied by height—one finds that the value of the consumer surplus in this example is actually 12.5.

Chapter 8

THEORY OF THE FIRM

The **theory of the consumer** is used to explain the market *demand* for goods and services. The **theory of the firm** provides an explanation for the market *supply* of goods and services. A **firm** is defined as any organization of individuals that purchases factors of production (labour, capital, and raw materials) in order to produce goods and services that are sold to consumers, governments, or other firms. The theory of the firm assumes that the firm's primary objective is to *maximize profits*. In maximizing profits, firms are subject to two constraints: the consumers' demand for their product and the costs of production. The discussion of how consumer demand affects firm decisions is taken up in later sections. This section focuses on the firm's production opportunities and cost constraints.

Production

Consider a firm that produces a single good. In order to produce this good, the firm must employ or purchase a number of different factors of production. The firm's **production decision** is to determine how much of each factor of production to employ.

Variable and fixed factors of production. In the **short-run,** some of the factors of production that the firm needs are available only in **fixed** quantities. For example, the size of the firm's factory, its machinery, and other capital equipment cannot be varied on a day-to-day basis. In the **long-run,** the firm can adjust the size of its factory and its use of machinery and equipment, but in the short-run, the quantities of these factors of production are considered fixed. The short-run is defined as the period during which changes in certain factors of production are not possible. The long-run is defined as the period during which *all* factors of production can be varied.

Other factors of production, however, are **variable** in the short-run. For example, the number of workers the firm employs or the quantities of raw materials the firm uses can be varied on a day-to-day basis. A factor of production that can be varied in the short-run is called a **variable factor of production.** A factor of production that cannot be varied in the short-run is called a **fixed factor of production.** In the short-run, a firm can increase its production of goods and services only by increasing its use of *variable* factors of production.

Total and marginal product. A firm combines its factors of production in order to produce goods or output. The total amount of output the firm produces, the firm's **total product,** depends on the quantities of factors that the firm purchases or employs. The **marginal product** of a factor of production is the change in the firm's total product that results from an increase in that factor by one unit, holding all other factors constant.

To better understand the concepts of total and marginal product, consider a firm that produces a certain good using only labour and capital as inputs. Assume that the amount of capital the firm uses is fixed at 1 unit. When the firm combines its fixed unit of capital with different quantities of labour, it is able to vary its output or total product. The change in the firm's total product, due to a 1-unit increase in labour input, is referred to as the **marginal product of labour.**

Table 8-1 provides a simple numerical example. When the firm combines its fixed unit of capital with one worker, its total product increases from 0 units to 5 units of the good. The marginal product of the first worker is therefore 5 (5 − 0 = 5). If the firm adds a second worker, its total product increases to 15; the marginal product of the second worker is therefore 10 (15 − 5 = 10). Continuing in this manner, it is possible to determine the marginal product of every worker that the firm hires.

Table 8-1   Marginal Product of Labour and Diminishing Returns

Labour input (workers)	Capital input (units)	Total product (number of goods)	Marginal product of labour
0	1	0	0
1	1	5	5
2	1	15	10
3	1	23	8
4	1	27	4
5	I	29	2
6	1	30	1

Law of diminishing returns. The **law of diminishing returns** says that as successive units of a variable factor of production are combined with fixed factors of production, the marginal product of the variable factor of production will eventually decline. The law of diminishing returns is illustrated in Table 8-1. As more and more workers are combined with the firm's fixed amount of capital, the marginal product of labour eventually starts to decline; in Table 8-1, diminishing returns "set in" beginning with the third worker. Intuitively, if the firm's capital is fixed at 1 unit, the production possibilities of the firm are limited. Adding more and more workers cannot alleviate this situation and will eventually cause the marginal product of additional workers to fall. Note that diminishing returns is a **short-run phenomenon** that will persist only as long as there are fixed factors of production; in the long-run, it will be possible to vary the amount of the fixed factor capital so as to eliminate the problem of diminishing returns.

Production Costs and Firm Profits

The firm's primary objective in producing output is to *maximize profits.* The production of output, however, involves certain *costs* that reduce the profits a firm can make. The relationship between costs and profits is therefore critical to the firm's determination of how much output to produce.

Explicit and implicit costs. A firm's **explicit costs** comprise all explicit payments to the factors of production the firm uses. Wages paid to workers, payments to suppliers of raw materials, and fees paid to bankers and lawyers are all included among the firm's explicit costs.

A firm's **implicit costs** consist of the **opportunity costs** of using the firm's own resources without receiving any explicit compensation for those resources. For example, a firm that uses its own building for production purposes foregoes the income that it might receive from renting the building out. As another example, consider the owner of a firm who works along with his employees but does not draw a salary; the owner forgoes the opportunity to earn a wage working for someone else. These implicit costs are not regarded as costs in an accounting sense, but they are a part of the firm's costs of doing business, nonetheless. When economists discuss *costs,* they have in mind *both* explicit and implicit costs.

Accounting profits, economic profits, and normal profits. The difference between explicit and implicit costs is crucial to understanding the difference between accounting profits and economic profits. **Accounting profits** are the firm's total revenues from sales of its output, minus the firm's explicit costs. **Economic profits** are total revenues minus explicit and implicit costs. Alternatively stated, economic profits are accounting profits minus implicit costs. Thus, the difference between economic profits and accounting profits is that economic profits include the firm's implicit costs and accounting profits do not.

A firm is said to make **normal profits** when its economic profits are *zero*. The fact that economic profits are zero implies that the firm's reserves are enough to cover the firm's explicit costs and all of its implicit costs, such as the rent that could be earned on the firm's building or the salary the owner of the firm could earn elsewhere. These implicit costs add up to the profits the firm would normally receive if it were properly compensated for the use of its own resources—hence the name, normal profits.

Fixed and variable costs. In the short-run, some of the input factors the firm uses in production are fixed. The cost of these fixed factors are the firm's fixed costs. The firm's fixed costs do not vary with increases in the firm's output.

The firm also employs a number of variable factors of production. The cost of these variable factors of production are the firm's **variable costs.** In order to increase output, the firm must increase the number of variable factors of production that it employs. Therefore, as firm output increases, the firm's variable costs must also increase.

To illustrate the concepts of fixed and variable costs, consider again the example of a single firm operating in the short-run with a fixed amount of capital, 1 unit, and a variable amount of labour. Suppose the cost of the single unit of capital is $100 and the cost of hiring each worker is $20. The firm's fixed and variable costs are reported in Table 8-2, which is a continuation of the numerical example presented in Table 8-1.

The first three columns of Table 8-2 correspond to the first three columns of Table 8-1. The fourth column of Table 8-2 reports the variable cost that the firm incurs from hiring 1 to 6 workers at $20 each, while the fifth column reports the fixed cost of the single unit of capital that the firm employs. The fixed cost of $100 is the same—no matter how many units of output the firm produces.

Table 8-2   Firm Output and Costs

Labour input	Capital input	Total product	Variable cost	Fixed cost	Total cost	Marginal cost
0	1	0	$0	$100	$100	—
1	1	5	20	100	120	$4.0
2	1	15	40	100	140	2.0
3	1	23	60	100	160	2.5
4	1	27	80	100	180	5.0
5	1	29	100	100	200	10.0
6	I	30	120	100	220	20.0

Total and marginal costs. The firm's **total cost** of production is the *sum of all its variable and fixed costs.* The firm's **marginal cost** is the *per unit change in total cost that results from a change in total product.* The concepts of total and marginal cost are illustrated in Table 8-2. The sixth column of this table reports the firm's total costs, which are simply the sum of its variable and fixed costs. The seventh column reports the marginal cost associated with different levels of output.

For example, when the firm increases its total product from 0 to 5 units of output, the change in the firm's total costs is $120 – $100 = $20. The marginal cost for the first 5 units of output is therefore $20/5 = $4. Similarly, when the firm increases its total product by 10 units, from 5 to 15 units of output, its total costs increase by $140 – $120 = $20. The marginal cost for the next 10 units produced is therefore $20/10 = $2.

Marginal cost and marginal product. The firm's **marginal cost** is related to its marginal product. If one calculates the change in total cost for each different level of total product reported and divides by the corresponding marginal product of labour reported in Table 8-1, one arrives at the marginal cost figure. Notice that the marginal cost falls at first, then starts to rise. This behaviour is a consequence of the relationship between marginal cost and marginal product and the law of diminishing returns. As the marginal product of the variable input—labour—*rises*, the firm's total product increases at a rate that is greater than the rate of new workers hired. Consequently, the firms marginal costs will be decreasing.

Eventually, however, by the law of diminishing returns, the marginal product of the variable factor will begin to decline; the firm's total product will increase at a rate less than the rate at which new workers are hired. The result is that the firm's marginal costs will begin rising.

Average variable, average fixed, and average total costs. The firm's variable, fixed, and total costs can all be calculated on an *average* or *per unit* basis. Table 8-3 reports the **average variable costs, average fixed costs,** and **average total costs** for the numerical example of Table 8-2.

Table 8-3   Firm Output and Average Costs

Total product	Average variable cost	Average fixed cost	Average total cost
0	—	—	—
5	$4.00	$20.00	$24.00
15	2.66	6.66	9.33
23	2.61	4.35	6.96
27	2.96	3.70	6.66
29	3.45	3.45	6.90
30	4.00	3.33	7.33

When the firm produces 27 units of output, for example, the firm's variable costs from Table 8-2 are $80. The *average* variable cost per unit of output is therefore $80/27 = $2.96, as reported in Table 8-3. The fixed cost corresponding to 27 units of output is $100; therefore, the average fixed cost per unit of output is $100/27 = $3.70. The total cost of 27 units of output is $180; so, the average total cost is $180/27 = $6.66.

Graphical depiction of costs. The variable, fixed, and total costs reported in Table 8-2 are shown in Figure 8-1(a). The marginal cost reported in Table 8-2 along with the average variable, average fixed, and average total costs reported in Table 8-3 are shown in the graph in Figure 8-1(b).

Figure 8-1 Cost curves

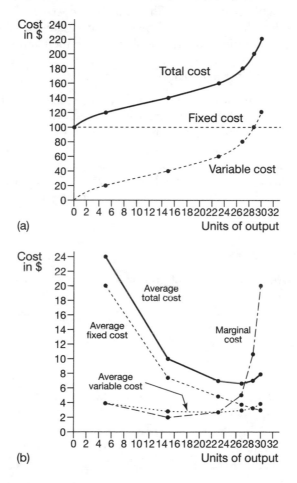

(a)

(b)

When costs are depicted graphically, they are referred to as **cost curves.** Figures 8-1(a) and 8-1(b) reveal some of the interesting relationships that exist among the various cost curves. Note first that the **total cost curve** is just the vertical summation of the **variable cost curve** and the **fixed cost curve.** This also holds true for the average **total cost curve,** which is just the vertical summation of the average **variable cost curve** and the **average fixed cost curve.**

Second, note the relationship between the marginal cost curve and the total and variable cost curves. The **marginal cost curve** reaches its *minimum* at the inflection point of the total and variable cost curves. This should not be surprising because the slope of the total and variable cost curves reveals the rate at which the firm's costs change as output increases, which is precisely what marginal cost measures.

Finally, notice that the marginal cost curve intersects both the average variable cost curve and the average total cost curve at the minimum points of both curves. This is in accordance with the **marginal-average rule,** which states that when marginal cost lies *below* average cost, average cost is *falling.* When marginal cost lies *above* average cost, average cost is *rising.* It follows, then, that the marginal cost curve will intersect the average variable and average total cost curves at each of these curves' minimum points.

Long-run Costs

In the short-run, some factors of production are fixed. Corresponding to each different level of fixed factors, there will be a different **short-run average total cost curve** *(SATC).* The average total cost curve, depicted in Figure 8-1(b), is just one of many *SATC*s that can be obtained by varying the amount of the fixed factor, in this case, the amount of capital.

Long-run average total cost curve. In the long-run, all factors of production are variable, and hence, all costs are variable. The **long-run average total cost curve** *(LATC)* is found by varying the amount of all factors of production. However, because each *SATC* corresponds to a different level of the fixed factors of production, the *LATC* can be constructed by taking the "lower envelope" of all the *SATC*s, as is illustrated in Figure 8-2.

The *LATC* is shown to be tangent to each of five different *SATC*s, labeled *SATC*$_1$ through *SATC*s. In general, there will be a large number of *SATC*s, each of which corresponds to a different level of the fixed factors the firm can employ in the short-run. Because there is such a large number of *SATC*s—more than just the five illustrated in Figure 8-2—the lower envelope of all the *SATC*s, which makes up the *LATC,* can be approximated by a smooth, U-shaped curve.

Figure 8-2 Short- and long-run average total cost curves

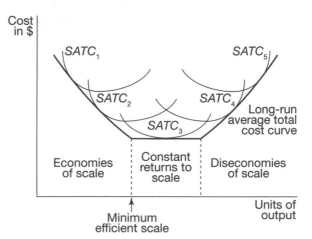

Economies of scale. The U-shape of the *LATC*, depicted in Figure 8-2, reflects the changing costs of production that the firm faces in the long-run as it varies the level of its factors of production and hence the level of its output. At low levels of output, a firm can usually increase its output at a rate that *exceeds* the rate at which it increases its factor inputs. When this situation occurs, the firm's average total costs are falling, and the firm is said to be experiencing **economies of scale.**

At higher levels of output, the firm may find that its output increases at the *same* rate at which it increases its factor inputs. In this case, the firm's average total costs remain constant, and the firm is said to experience **constant returns to scale.** At even higher output levels, the firm's output will tend to increase at a rate that is *below* the rate at which it increases its factor inputs. In this situation, average total costs are rising, and the firm is said to experience **diseconomies of scale.**

The firm's **minimum efficient** scale is the level of output at which economies of scale end and constant returns to scale begin. The minimum efficient scale is indicated in Figure 8-2.

Chapter 9

PERFECT COMPETITION

When economists analyze the production decisions of a firm, they take into account the structure of the market in which the firm is operating. The structure of the market is determined by four different market characteristics: the number and size of the firms in the market, the ease with which firms may enter and exit the market, the degree to which firms' products are differentiated, and the amount of information available to both buyers and sellers regarding prices, product characteristics, and production techniques.

Economists distinguish among four different **market structures,** which they refer to as **perfect competition, monopoly, monopolistic competition,** and **oligopoly.** This section considers the case of a firm operating in a perfectly competitive market structure, while the next two sections consider the behaviour of firms operating under the other three types of market structures.

Conditions for Perfect Competition

Four characteristics or conditions must be present for a perfectly competitive market structure to exist. First, there must be *many firms* in the market, none of which is large in terms of its sales. Second, firms should be able to *enter and exit the market easily.* Third, each firm in the market produces and sells a nondifferentiated or *homogeneous product.* Fourth, all firms and consumers in the market have *complete information* about prices, product quality, and production techniques.

Price-taking behaviour. A firm that is operating in a perfectly competitive market will be a **price-taker.** A price-taker cannot control the price of the good it sells; it simply takes the market price as given. The conditions that cause a market to be perfectly competitive also cause the firms in that market to be price-takers. When there are many firms, all producing and selling the same product using the same inputs and technology, competition forces each firm to charge the same market price for its good. Because each firm in the market sells the same, homogeneous product, no single firm can increase the price that it charges above the price charged by the other firms in the market without losing business. It is also impossible for a single firm to affect the market price by changing the quantity of output it supplies because, by assumption, there are many firms and each firm is small in size.

Demand in a Perfectly Competitive Market

The demand and supply curves for a perfectly competitive market are illustrated in Figure 9-1(a); the demand curve for the output of an individual firm operating in this perfectly competitive market is illustrated in Figure 9-1(b).

Figure 9-1   Market and firm demand curves in a perfectly competitive market

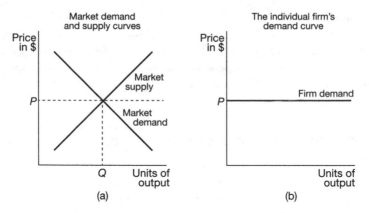

Note that the demand curve for the market, which includes all firms, is *downward sloping,* while the demand curve for the individual firm is flat or *perfectly elastic,* reflecting the fact that the individual takes the market price, *P*, as given. The difference in the slopes of the market demand curve and the individual firm's demand curve is due to the assumption that each firm is small in size. No matter how much output an individual firm provides, it will be unable to affect the market price. Note that the individual firm's equilibrium quantity of output will be completely determined by the amount of output the individual firm chooses to supply.

Short-run Supply in a Perfectly Competitive Market

In determining how much output to supply, the firm's objective is to maximize profits subject to two constraints: the consumers' demand for the firm's product and the firm's costs of production. Consumer demand determines the price at which a perfectly competitive firm may sell its output. The costs of production are determined by the technology the firm uses. The firm's profits are the difference between its total revenues and total costs.

Total revenue and marginal revenue. A firm's **total revenue** is the dollar amount that the firm earns *from* sales of its output. If a firm decides to supply the amount Q of output and the price in the perfectly competitive market is P, the firm's total revenue is

$$P \times Q$$

A firm's **marginal revenue** is the dollar amount by which its total revenue changes in response to a 1-unit change in the firm's output. If a firm in a perfectly competitive market increases its output by 1 unit, it increases its total revenue by $P \times 1 = P$. Hence, in a perfectly competitive market, the firms marginal revenue is just equal to the market price, P.

Short-run profit maximization. A firm maximizes its profits by choosing to supply the level of output where its marginal revenue equals its marginal cost. When marginal revenue exceeds marginal cost, the firm can earn greater profits by increasing its output. When marginal revenue is below marginal cost, the firm is losing money, and consequently, it must reduce its output. Profits are therefore maximized when the firm chooses the level of output where its marginal revenue equals its marginal cost.

To illustrate the concept of profit maximization, consider again the example of the firm that produces a single good using only two inputs, labour and capital. In the short-run, the amount of capital the firm uses is fixed at 1 unit. Assume that this firm is competing with many other firms in a perfectly competitive market. The price of the good sold in this market is $10 per unit. The firm's costs of production for different levels of output are the same as those considered in the numerical examples of the previous section, Theory of the Firm. These costs, along with the firm's total and marginal revenues and its profits for different levels of output, are reported in Table 9-1.

Table 9-1   Firm Output, Revenues, Costs, and Profits

Total product	Total revenue	Marginal revenue	Total cost	Average total cost	Marginal cost	Firm profits
0	$0	—	$100	—	—	−$100
5	50	$10	120	$24.00	$4.0	−70
15	150	10	140	9.33	2.0	10
23	230	10	160	6.96	2.5	70
27	270	10	180	6.66	5.0	90
29	290	10	200	6.90	10.0	90
30	300	10	220	7.33	20.0	80

Because the price of the good is $10, the firm's total revenue is 10 x total product. The firm's marginal revenue is equal to the price of $10 per unit of total product. Notice that the marginal cost of the 29th unit produced is $10, while the marginal revenue from the 29th unit is also $10. Hence, the firm maximizes its profits by choosing to produce exactly 29 units of output. In choosing to produce 29 units of output, the firm earns $90 ($290 − 200) in profits.

Graphical illustration of short-run profit maximization. The marginal revenue, marginal cost, and average total cost figures reported in the numerical example of Table 9-1 are shown in the graph in Figure 9-2.

The firm's equilibrium supply of 29 units of output is determined by the intersection of the marginal cost and marginal revenue curves (point *d* in Figure 9-2). When the firm produces 29 units of output, its average total cost is found to be $6.90 (point *c* on the average total cost curve in Figure 9-2). The firm's profits are therefore given by the area of the shaded rectangle labeled *abcd*.

The area of this rectangle is easily calculated. The length of the rectangle is 29. The width is the difference between the market price (the firm's marginal revenue), $10, and the firm's average cost of producing 29 units, $6.90. This difference is ($10 − *$6.90*) = $3.10. Hence, the area of rectangle *abcd* is 29 x $3.1 = $90, the same amount reported in Table 9-1. In general, the firm makes positive profits whenever its average total cost curve lies *below* its marginal revenue curve.

Figure 9-2 The firm's short-run, profit-maximizing decision

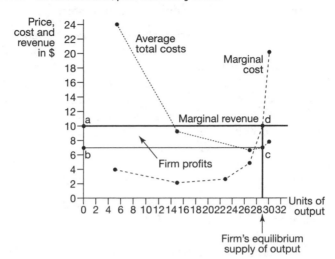

Firm's equilibrium
supply of output

Short-run losses and the shut-down decision. When the firm's average total cost curve lies *above* its marginal revenue curve at the profit maximizing level of output, the firm is experiencing *losses* and will have to consider whether to shut down its operations. In making this determination, the firm will take into account its **average variable** costs rather than its **average total costs.** The difference between the firm's *average* total costs and its average variable costs is its **average fixed costs.** The firm must pay its fixed costs (for example, its purchases of factory space and equipment), *regardless* of whether it produces any output. Hence, the firm's fixed costs are considered sunk costs and will not have any bearing on whether the firm decides to shut down. Thus, the firm will focus on its average variable costs in determining whether to shut down.

If the firm's average variable costs are *less* than its marginal revenue at the profit maximizing level of output, the firm *will not shut down in the short-run.* The firm is better off continuing its operations because it can cover its variable costs and use any remaining revenues to pay off some of its fixed costs. The fact that the firm can pay its variable costs is all that matters because in the short-run, the firm's fixed costs are sunk; the firm must pay its fixed costs regardless of whether or not it decides to shut down. Of course, the firm will not continue to incur losses indefinitely. In the long-run, a firm that is incurring losses will have to either shut down or reduce its fixed costs by changing its fixed factors of production in a manner that makes the firm's operations profitable.

The case where the firm is incurring short-run losses but continues to operate is illustrated graphically in Figure 9-3(a). At the market price, P_1, the firm's profit maximizing quantity is Q_1. At this quantity, the firm's average total cost curve lies *above* its marginal revenue curve, which is the flat, dashed line denoting the price level, P_1. The firm's average variable cost curve, however, lies *below* its marginal revenue curve, implying that the firm *is able* to cover its variable costs. The firm's *losses* from producing quantity Q_1 at price P_1 are given by the area of the rectangle *abcd*. Despite these losses, the firm will decide not to shut down in the short-run because it receives enough revenue to pay for its variable costs.

Figure 9-3(b) depicts a different scenario in which the firm's average total cost and average variable cost curves *both lie above* its marginal revenue curve, which is the dashed line at price P_2. The firm's *losses* are given by the area of the rectangle *abcd*. In this situation, the firm *will have to shut down in the short-run* because it is unable to cover even its variable costs. As a general rule, a firm will shut down production whenever its average variable costs exceed its marginal revenue at the profit maximizing level of output. If this is not the case, the firm may continue its operations in the short-run, even though it may be experiencing losses.

Figure 9-3   The firm's short-run shut-down decision

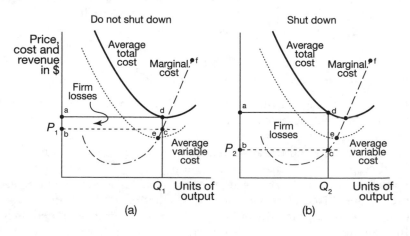

(a)

(b)

Short-run supply curve. The firm's **short-run supply curve** is the portion of its marginal cost curve that lies *above* its average variable cost curve. As the market price rises, the firm will supply more of its product, in accordance with the law of supply. If, however, the market price, which is the firm's marginal revenue curve, falls below the firm's average variable cost, the firm will shut down and supply zero output.

The **firm's short-run supply curve** is illustrated in Figures 9-3(a) and 9-3(b). Here, the firm's short-run supply *curve* is the portion of the marginal cost curve labeled *ef.* The **market short-run supply curve,** like the market demand curve, is simply the horizontal summation of all the individual firms' short-run supply curves.

Long-run Supply in a Perfectly Competitive Market

In the long-run, firms can vary all of their input factors. The ability to vary the amount of input factors in the long-run allows for the possibility that *new firms will enter* the market and that *some existing firms will exit* the market. Recall that in a perfectly competitive market, there are *no barriers to* the entry and exit of firms. New firms will be tempted to enter the market if some of the existing firms in the market are earning **positive economic profits.** Alternatively, existing firms may choose to leave the market if they are earning losses. For these reasons, the number of firms in a perfectly competitive market is unlikely to remain unchanged in the long-run.

Zero economic profits. The entry and exit of firms, which is possible in the long-run, will eventually cause each firm's *economic profits* to fall to *zero.* Hence, in the long-run each firm earns **normal profits.** If some firms are earning *positive* economic profits in the short-run, in the long-run new firms will enter the market and the increased competition will reduce all firms' economic profits to zero. Firms that are earning negative economic profits (losses) in the short-run will have to either make some changes in their fixed factors of production in the long-run or choose to leave the market in the long-run. A perfectly competitive market achieves **long-run equilibrium** when all firms are earning zero economic profits and when the number of firms in the market is not changing.

Minimization of long-run average total cost. In the long-run, a perfectly competitive firm can adjust the amount it uses of *all* factor inputs, including those that are fixed in the short-run. For example, in the long-run, the firm can adjust the size of its factory. In making these adjustments, the firm will seek to *minimize* its long-run average total cost. If, in the short-run, the firm is operating *below* its minimum efficient scale and experiencing **economies of scale,** in the long-run it can adjust its use of factor inputs so as to *increase* its output to the minimum efficient scale level.

Alternatively, if the firm is experiencing **diseconomies** of scale because its short-run level of output *exceeds* its minimum efficient scale, in the long-run the firm can adjust its use of factor inputs so as to *reduce* its output to the minimum efficient scale level. Thus, in the long-run the firm will be operating at the minimum point of its long-run average total cost curve.

Graphical illustration of long-run profit maximization. The long-run equilibrium for an individual firm in a perfectly competitive market is illustrated in Figure 9-4.

Figure 9-4   The firm's long-run profit-maximizing decision

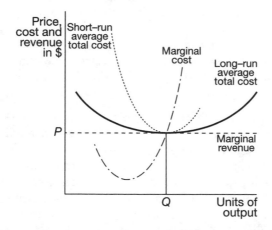

The profit maximizing level of output, where marginal cost equals marginal revenue, results in an equilibrium quantity of Q units of output. Because the firm's average total costs per unit equal the firm's marginal revenue per unit, the firm is earning zero economic profits.

Furthermore, the firm is shown to be producing at the minimum point of its long-run average total cost curve. At the minimum efficient scale level of output.

Long-run market supply curve. The short-run market supply curve is just the horizontal summation of all the individual firm's supply curves. The **long-run market supply curve** is found by examining the responsiveness of short-run market supply to a change in market demand. Consider the market demand and supply curves depicted in Figures 9-5(a) and 9-5(b). Here, the market demand curves are labeled D_1 and D_2, while the short-run market supply curves are labeled S_1 and S_2.

Figure 9-5(a) depicts demand and supply curves for a market or industry in which firms face **constant costs** of production as output increases. At the intersection of D_1 and S_1, the market is in long-run equilibrium at a market price of P_1. An increase in demand from D_1 to D_2 results in a new, higher market price of P_2. In the short-run, existing firms in this market will earn positive economic profits. In the long-run, however, new firms will enter, causing short-run market supply to shift from S_1 to S_2 and driving the market price back down to P_1. The long-run market supply curve is therefore given by the horizontal line at the market price, P_1.

Figure 9-5 Long-run market supply curves

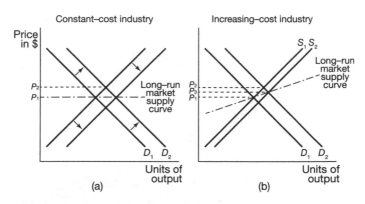

(a)

(b)

Figure 9-5(b) depicts demand and supply curves for a market or industry in which firms face *increasing costs* of production as output increases. Starting from a market price of P_1, an increase in demand from D_1 to D_2 increases the market price to P_2. In the short-run, firms are earning positive economic profits. In the long-run, new firms will enter the market, the short-run supply curve will shift from S_1 to S_2, and the new market price will be P_3. The new, long-run market price of P_3 is greater than the old market price of P, because in an increasing-cost industry, the firm's average total costs *rise* as it produces more output. Thus, the long-run market supply curve in an increasing-cost industry will be *positively sloped*.

Chapter 10

MONOPOLY

In a perfectly competitive market, there are many firms, none of which is large in size. In contrast, in a **monopolistic** market there is only *one* firm, which is large in size. This one firm provides all of the market's supply. Hence, in a monopolistic market, there is *no difference* between the firm's supply and market supply.

Conditions for Monopoly

Three conditions characterize a monopolistic market structure. First, as mentioned above, there is *only one firm* operating in the market. Second, there are *high barriers to entry*. These barriers are so high that they prevent any other firm from entering the market. Third, there are *no close substitutes* for the good the monopoly firm produces. Because there are no close substitutes, the monopoly does not face any competition.

Barriers to entry. A barrier to entry is anything that prevents firms from entering a market. Many types of barriers to entry give rise to a monopolistic market structure. Some of the more common barriers to entry are

1. **Patents:** If a firm holds a patent on a production process, it can legally exclude other firms from using that process for a number of years. If there are no other production processes that can be used, the firm that holds the patent will have a monopoly.

2. **Large start-up costs:** In some markets, firms will face large start-up costs—for example, the cost of building a new production facility. If these start-up costs are large enough, most firms will be discouraged from entering the market.

3. **Limited access to resources:** A monopolistic market structure is likely to arise when access to resources needed for production is limited. The market for diamonds, for example, is dominated by a single firm that owns most of the world's diamond mines.

Natural monopolies. Not all monopolies arise from these kinds of barriers to entry. A few monopolies arise *naturally,* in markets where there are large economies of scale. For example, a local telephone company's marginal and average costs tend to decline as it adds more customers; as the company increases its network of telephone lines, it costs the company less and less to add additional customers. The telephone company's long-run average costs may eventually rise but only at a level of output that is beyond the level the local market demands. Hence, in the market for local telephone services, there is a need for only one firm; competition will not naturally arise. Gas, electric power, and other local utilities are also examples of natural monopolies.

Demand in a Monopolistic Market

Because the monopolist is the market's only supplier, the demand curve the monopolist faces is the **market demand curve.** You will recall that the market demand curve is *downward sloping,* reflecting the law of demand. The fact that the monopolist faces a downward-sloping demand *curve* implies that the price a monopolist can expect to receive for its output will not remain constant as the monopolist increases its output.

Price-searching behaviour. Unlike a perfectly competitive firm, the monopolist does not have to simply take the market price as given. Instead, the monopolist is a **price searcher;** it searches the market demand curve for the **profit maximizing price.** The monopolist's search for the profit maximizing price involves comparing the marginal revenue and marginal cost associated with each possible price-output combination on the market demand curve.

Declining marginal revenue and price. The monopolist's marginal revenue from each unit sold does not remain constant as in the case of the perfectly competitive firm. As mentioned above, the monopolist faces the downward-sloping *market* demand curve, so the price that the monopolist can get for each additional unit of output must fall as the monopolist increases its output. Consequently, the monopolist's *marginal revenue* will also be falling as the monopolist increases its output. If it is assumed that the monopolist cannot *price discriminate,* that is, charge a different price for each unit of output it produces, then the monopolist's marginal revenue from each additional unit produced *will not* equal the price that the monopolist charges. In fact, the marginal revenue that the monopolist receives from producing an additional unit of output will always *be less* than the price that the monopolist can charge for the additional unit.

To understand why, consider a monopolist that is currently supplying N units of output. Suppose the monopolist decides to supply 1 more unit. It therefore increases its supply to $N + 1$ units of output. The downward-sloping market demand curve indicates that the new market price will be *lower* than before. Because the monopolist cannot price discriminate, it will have to sell all $N + 1$ units of output at the new lower price. This new lower price *reduces* the *total revenue* that the monopolist receives from the first N units sold. At the same time, the monopolist will gain some revenue from the additional unit it supplies. The marginal revenue that the monopolist receives from supplying 1 additional unit is equal to the price that it receives for this unit minus its loss in revenue from having to sell N units of output at a lower market price. Thus, the price the monopolist receives from selling $N + 1$ units exceeds the marginal revenue that it receives from supplying the additional unit of output.

The relationship between marginal revenue and price in a monopolistic market is best understood by considering a numerical example, such as the one provided in Table 10-1.

Table 10-1   Market Demand and Monopoly Revenue

Output	Price	Total revenue	Marginal revenue
0	$14	$0	—
1	12	12	$12
2	10	20	8
3	8	24	4
4	6	24	0
5	4	20	−4

The first two columns of Table 10-1, labeled "Output" and "Price," represent the **market demand schedule** that the monopolist faces. As the price falls, the market's demand for output increases, in keeping with the law of demand. The third column reports the total revenue that the monopolist receives from each different level of output. The fourth column reports the monopolist's marginal revenue that is just the change in total revenue per 1 unit change of output. Note that the monopolist's marginal revenue is declining as output increases, in accordance with the discussion above.

Suppose the monopolist is currently producing 2 units of output for which it is receiving a price of $10 per unit and a total revenue of $20 (2 x $10). Now, consider what happens when the monopolist increases its output to 3 units. The price that the monopolist can expect to receive falls to $8 per unit. At this new lower price, the total revenue the monopolist receives for the first two units of output it supplies falls from $20 to $16 (2 x $8), a loss of $4. The monopolist's marginal revenue is equal to the $8 that it receives from the third unit sold minus the loss in total revenue that it receives on the first two units due to the new lower price. Hence, the marginal revenue the monopolist receives from the third unit sold is $8 − $4 = $4, which is below the market price of $8.

Profit Maximization in a Monopolistic Market

The monopolist's profit maximizing level of output is found by equating its marginal revenue with its marginal cost, which is the same profit maximizing condition that a perfectly competitive firm uses to determine its equilibrium level of output. Indeed, the condition that marginal revenue equal marginal cost is used to determine the profit maximizing level of output of *every firm, regardless of the market structure* in which the firm is operating.

In order to determine the profit maximizing level of output, the monopolist will need to supplement its information about market demand and prices with data on its costs of production for different levels of output. As an example of the costs that a monopolist might face, consider the data in Table 10-2, which is a continuation of the numerical example of Table 10-1. The data from Table 10-1 are rewritten as the first four columns of Table 10-2. The fifth column of Table 10-2 reports the monopolist's total cost of providing 0 to 5 units of output. The sixth and seventh columns report the monopolist's average total costs and marginal costs per unit of output. The eighth column reports the monopolist's profits, which is the difference between total revenue and total cost at each level of output.

The monopolist will choose to produce 3 units of output because the marginal revenue that it receives from the third unit of output, $4, is equal to the marginal cost of producing the third unit of output, $4. The monopolist will earn $12 in profits from producing 3 units of output, the maximum possible.

Table 10-2   Monopoly Output, Revenues, Costs, and Profits

Output	Price	Total revenue	Marginal revenue	Total cost	Average total cost	Marginal cost	Monopoly profits
0	$14	$0	—	$2	—	—	−2
1	12	12	$12	6	$6	$4	6
2	10	20	8	8	4	2	12
3	8	24	4	12	4	4	12
4	6	24	0	20	5	8	4
5	4	20	−4	35	7	15	−15

Graphical illustration of monopoly profit maximization. Figure 10-1 illustrates the monopolist's profit maximizing decision using the data given in Table 10-2. Note that the **market demand curve,** which represents the *price* the monopolist can expect to receive at every level of output, lies above the **marginal revenue curve,** in accordance with the discussion above.

The result of the monopolist's price searching is a price of $8 per unit. This equilibrium price is determined by finding the profit maximizing level of output—where marginal revenue equals marginal cost (point *c*)—and then looking at the demand curve to find the price at which the profit maximizing level of output will be demanded. The monopolist's profit-maximizing decision

Monopoly profits and losses. The monopoly in the example above made profits of $12. These profits are illustrated in Figure 10-1 as the rectangle labeled *abcd*. While you usually think of monopolists as earning positive economic profits, this is not always the case. Monopolists, like perfectly competitive firms, can also incur losses in the short-run. Monopolists will experience short-run losses whenever average total costs exceed the price that the monopolist can charge at the profit maximizing level of output.

Figure 10-1 The monopolist's profit-maximizing decision

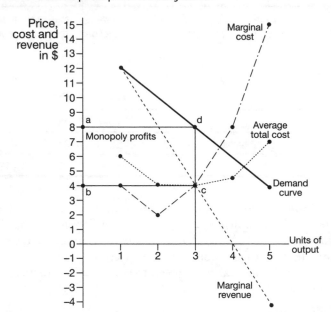

Absence of a monopoly supply curve. In Figure 10-1, there is no representation of the monopolist's supply curve. In fact, the monopolist's supply schedule cannot be depicted as a supply curve that is independent of the market demand curve. Whereas a perfectly competitive firm's supply curve is equal to a portion of its marginal cost curve, the monopolist's supply decisions do not depend on marginal cost alone. The monopolist looks at both the marginal cost and the marginal revenue that it receives at each price level. In order to determine marginal revenue, the monopolist must know market demand. Therefore, the monopolist's market supply will not be independent of market demand.

Monopoly in the Long-run

In the discussion of a perfectly competitive market structure, a distinction was made between short-run and long-run market behaviour. In the long-run, all input factors are assumed to be variable, making it possible for firms to enter and exit the market. The consequence of this entry and exit of firms was that each firm's economic profits *were* reduced to zero in the long-run.

The distinction between the short-run and the long-run is not as important in the case of a monopolistic market structure. The existence of high barriers to entry prevents firms from entering the market even in the long-run. Therefore, it is possible for the monopolist to avoid competition and continue making *positive* economic profits in the long-run.

Costs of Monopoly

A monopolist produces *less output* and sells it at a *higher price* than a perfectly competitive firm. The monopolist's behaviour is costly to the consumers who demand the monopolist's output. The cost of monopoly that is borne by consumers is illustrated in Figure 10-2. The firm's marginal cost curve is drawn as a horizontal line at the market price of $5.

In a perfectly competitive market, the firm's marginal revenue curve is also equal to the market price of $5. Therefore, total output in a perfectly competitive market will be 5 units. In a monopolistic market, however, marginal revenue and marginal cost intersect at 3 units of output. The monopolist sells its output at $7 per unit—the price on the market demand curve that corresponds to 3 units of output.

Figure 10-2 Costs of monopoly

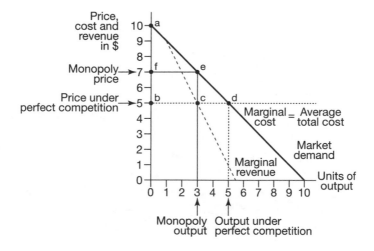

The cost to the consumer of a monopolistic market structure is the **reduction in consumer surplus** that results from monopoly output and price decisions. Under perfect competition, consumer surplus is given by the area of triangle, *abd,* in Figure 10-2. Under monopoly, this consumer surplus is *reduced* by the area of the trapezoid, *fedb.* Of this amount, the amount represented by *fecb,* now accrues to the monopolist; *edc* is the deadweight loss resulting from the monopolist charging a higher, inefficient price. Consumer losses from monopolistic markets have resulted in legal efforts to break up monopolies and government regulation of natural monopolies.

Chapter 11

MONOPOLISTIC COMPETITION AND OLIGOPOLY

Perfect competition and pure monopoly represent the two extreme possibilities for a market's structure. The structure of almost all markets, however, falls somewhere *between* these two extremes. This section considers two market structures, **monopolistic competition** and **oligopoly,** which lie between the extreme cases of perfect competition and monopoly. Monopolistic competition, as its name suggests, is a combination of monopoly and competition. However, monopolistic competition is more closely related to perfect competition than to monopoly. Oligopoly is also a combination of monopoly and competition, but it is more closely related to monopoly than to perfect competition.

Conditions for a Monopolistically Competitive Market

Three conditions characterize a **monopolistically competitive market.** First, the market has *many firms, none* of which is *large.* Second, there is *free entry and exit* into the market; there are *no barriers* to entry or exit. Third, each firm in the market produces a *differentiated product.* This last condition is what distinguishes monopolistic competition from perfect competition. Examples of monopolistically competitive firms include restaurants, retail clothing stores, and gasoline service stations.

Differentiated products and monopolistic behaviour. In many markets, competing firms sell products that can be *differentiated* from one another. A firm's product can be differentiated in a number of different ways: by its quality, its convenience, its size, its colour, its look, its taste— even by its brand name! As a firm's product becomes more and more differentiated, the firm faces less and less competition and will be able to act more like a monopolist in its output and pricing decisions. Thus, in a monopolistically competitive industry, firms seek to differentiate their products as much as possible. Much of this differentiation is accomplished through **advertising.**

Demand in a Monopolistically Competitive Market

Because the monopolistically competitive firm's product is differentiated from other products, the firm will face is own downward-sloping "market" demand curve. This demand curve will be considerably more *elastic* than the demand curve that a monopolist faces because the monopolistically competitive firm has *less* control over the price that it can charge for its output. The firm's control over its price will depend on the degree to which its product is differentiated from competing firms' products. If the firm's product is not differentiated from other products, the firm will face a relatively *elastic* demand curve and will have less control over the price it can charge. If the firm's product is differentiated compared to a competing firm's products, the firm will face a relatively *inelastic* demand curve and will have more control over the price that it can charge.

Price-searching behaviour. The monopolistically competitive firm will be a **price-searcher** rather than a price-taker because it faces a downward-sloping demand curve for its product. The firm searches for the price that it will charge in the same way that a monopolist does, by comparing marginal revenue with marginal cost at each possible price along the market demand curve.

Profit Maximization by a Monopolistically Competitive Firm

An illustration of the monopolistically competitive firm's profit-maximizing decision is provided in Figure 11-1.

Figure 11-1   Short-run profit maximization by a monopolistically competitive firm

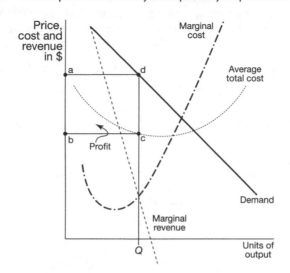

The firm maximizes its profits by equating marginal cost with marginal revenue. The intersection of the marginal cost and marginal revenue curves determines the firm's equilibrium level of output, labeled Q in this figure. The firm finds the price that it can charge for this level of output by looking at the market demand curve; if it provides Q units of output, it can charge a price of $P per unit of output. The firm is shown earning positive economic profits equal to the area of the rectangular box, *abcd*. Negative economic profits (losses) are also possible.

The monopolistically competitive firm's behaviour appears to be *no different* from the behaviour of a monopolist. In fact, in the short-run, there is no difference between the behaviour of a monopolistically competitive firm and a monopolist. However, in the long-run, an important difference does emerge.

Monopolistic Competition in the Long-run

The difference between the short-run and the long-run in a monopolistically competitive market is that in the long-run new firms can enter the market, which is especially likely if firms are earning positive economic profits in the short-run. New firms will be attracted to these profit opportunities and will choose to enter the market in the long-run. In contrast to a monopolistic market, no barriers to entry exist in a monopolistically competitive market; hence, it is quite easy for new firms to enter the market in the long-run.

The monopolistically competitive firm's long-run equilibrium situation is illustrated in Figure 11-2.

Figure 11-2    Long-run profit maximization by a monopolistically competitive firm

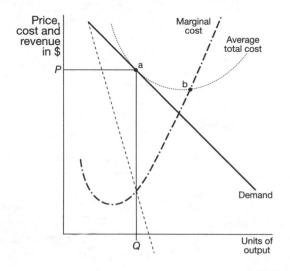

The entry of new firms leads to an *increase* in the supply of differentiated products, which causes the firm's market demand curve to shift to the *left*. As entry into the market increases, the firm's demand curve will continue shifting to the left until it is just tangent to the average total cost curve at the profit maximizing level of output, as shown in Figure 11-2. At this point, the firm's economic profits are zero, and there is no longer any incentive for new firms to enter the market. Thus, in the long-run, the competition brought about by the entry of new firms will cause each firm in a monopolistically competitive market to earn normal profits, just like a perfectly competitive firm.

Excess capacity. Unlike a perfectly competitive firm, a monopolistically competitive firm ends up choosing a level of output that is *below* its minimum efficient scale, labeled as point *b* in Figure 11-2. When the firm produces below its minimum efficient scale, it is under-utilizing its available resources. In this situation, the firm is said to have **excess capacity** because it can easily accommodate an increase in production. This excess capacity is the major social cost of a monopolistically competitive market structure.

Conditions for an Oligopolistic Market

Oligopoly is the least understood market structure; consequently, it has no single, unified theory. Nevertheless, there is some agreement as to what constitutes an oligopolistic market. Three conditions for oligopoly have been identified. First, an oligopolistic market has only a *few large firms.* This condition distinguishes oligopoly from monopoly, in which there is just one firm. Second, an oligopolistic market has *high barriers to entry.* This condition distinguishes oligopoly from perfect competition and monopolistic competition in which there are no barriers to entry. Third, oligopolistic firms may *produce either differentiated or homogeneous products.* Examples of oligopolistic firms include automobile manufacturers, oil producers, steel manufacturers, and passenger airlines.

Kinked-Demand Theory of Oligopoly

As mentioned above, there is no single theory of oligopoly. The two that are most frequently discussed, however, are the **kinked-demand theory** and the **cartel theory.** The kinked-demand theory is illustrated in Figure 11-3 and applies to oligopolistic markets where each firm sells a **differentiated product.** According to the kinked-demand theory, each firm will face *two market demand curves* for its product. At *high* prices, the firm faces the relatively *elastic* market demand curve, labeled MD_1 in Figure 11-3.

Corresponding to MD_1 is the marginal revenue curve labeled MR_1. At *low* prices, the firm faces the relatively *inelastic* market demand curve labeled MD_2. Corresponding to MD_2 is the marginal revenue curve labeled MR_2.

Figure 11-3 Profit maximization by an oligopolistic firm facing a kinked-demand curve

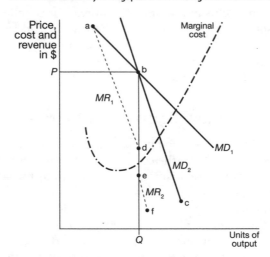

The two market demand curves intersect at point b. Therefore, the market demand curve that the oligopolist actually faces is the **kinked-demand curve,** labeled *abc.* Similarly, the marginal revenue that the oligopolist actually receives is represented by the marginal revenue curve labeled *adef.* The oligopolist maximizes profits by equating marginal revenue with marginal cost, which results in an equilibrium output of Q units and an equilibrium price *of P.*

The oligopolist faces a kinked-demand curve because of *competition* from other oligopolists in the market. If the oligopolist *increases* its price above the equilibrium price P, it is assumed that the other oligopolists in the market *will not* follow with price increases of their own. The oligopolist will then face the more elastic market demand curve MD_1.

The oligopolist's market demand curve becomes more elastic at prices above P because at these higher prices consumers are more likely to switch to the lower-priced products provided by the other oligopolists in the market. Consequently, the demand for the oligopolist's output falls off more quickly at prices above P; in other words, the demand for the oligopolist's output becomes more elastic.

If the oligopolist reduces its price *below P*, it is assumed that its competitors *will follow suit* and *reduce* their prices as well. The oligopolist will then face the relatively less elastic (or more inelastic) market demand curve MD_2. The oligopolist's market demand curve becomes less elastic at prices below P because the other oligopolists in the market have also reduced their prices. When oligopolists follow each other's pricing decisions, consumer demand for each oligopolist's product will become less elastic (or less sensitive) to changes in price because each oligopolist is matching the price changes of its competitors.

The kinked-demand theory of oligopoly illustrates the high degree of **interdependence** that exists among the firms that make up an oligopoly. The market demand curve that each oligopolist faces is determined by the output and price decisions of the other firms in the oligopoly; this is the major contribution of the kinked-demand theory. The kinked-demand theory, however, is considered an *incomplete* theory of oligopoly for several reasons. First, it does not explain how the oligopolist finds the kinked point in its market demand curve. Second, the kinked-demand theory does not allow for the possibility that price *increases* by one oligopolist are matched by other oligopolists, a practice that has been frequently observed. Finally, the kinked-demand theory does not consider the possibility that oligopolists *collude* in setting output and price. The possibility of collusive behavior is captured in the alternative theory known as the cartel theory of oligopoly.

Cartel Theory of Oligopoly

A **cartel** is defined as a group of firms that gets together to make output and price decisions. The conditions that give rise to an oligopolistic market are also conducive to the formation of a cartel; in particular, cartels tend to arise in markets where there are few firms and each firm has a significant share of the market. In the U.S., cartels are illegal; however, internationally, there are no restrictions on cartel formation. The organization of petroleum-exporting countries (OPEC) is perhaps the best-known example of an international cartel; OPEC members meet regularly to decide how much oil each member of the cartel will be allowed to produce.

Oligopolistic firms join a cartel to increase their market power, and members work together to determine jointly the level of output that each member will produce and/or the price that each member will charge. By working together, the cartel members are able to behave like a monopolist. For example, if each firm in an oligopoly sells an undifferentiated product like oil, the demand curve that each firm faces will be horizontal at the market price. If, however, the oil-producing firms form a cartel like OPEC to determine their output and price, they will jointly face a downward-sloping market demand curve, just like a monopolist. In fact, the cartel's profit-maximizing decision is the same as that of a monopolist, as Figure 11-4 reveals. The cartel members choose their combined output at the level where their combined marginal revenue equals their combined marginal cost. The cartel price is determined by market demand curve at the level of output chosen by the cartel. The cartel's profits are equal to the area of the rectangular box labeled *abcd* in Figure 11-4. Note that a cartel, like a monopolist, will choose to produce less output and charge a higher price than would be found in a perfectly competitive market.

Figure 11-4 Profit maximization by oligopolistic cartel

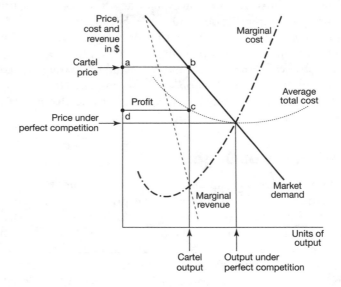

Once established, cartels are difficult to maintain. The problem is that cartel members will be tempted to cheat on their agreement to limit production. By producing more output than it has agreed to produce, a cartel member can increase its share of the cartel's profits. Hence, there is a built-in incentive for each cartel member to cheat. Of course, if all members cheated, the cartel would cease to earn monopoly profits, and there would no longer be any incentive for firms to remain in the cartel. The cheating problem has plagued the OPEC cartel as well as other cartels and perhaps explains why so few cartels exist.

Chapter 12

LABOUR MARKET

In addition to making output and pricing decisions, firms must also determine how much of each **input** to demand. Firms may choose to demand many different kinds of inputs. The two most common are **labour** and **capital**. This section considers the demand and supply of labour; the next considers the demand and supply of capital.

Labour Demand and Supply in a Perfectly Competitive Market

The demand and supply of labour are determined in the **labour market.** The participants in the labour market are **workers** and **firms.** Workers **supply** labour to firms in exchange for **wages.** Firms **demand** labour from workers in exchange for wages.

The firm's demand for labour. The **firm's demand for labour** is a **derived demand;** it is derived from the demand for the firm's **output.** If demand for the firm's output increases, the firm will demand more labour and will hire more workers. If demand for the firm's output falls, the firm will demand less labour and will reduce its work force.

Marginal revenue product of labour. When the firm knows the level of demand for its output, it determines how much labour to demand by looking at the **marginal revenue product of labour.** The marginal revenue product of labour (or any input) is the additional revenue the firm earns by employing one more unit of labour. The marginal revenue product of labour is related to the **marginal product of labour.** In a perfectly competitive market, the firm's marginal revenue product of labour is the **value of the marginal product of labour.**

For example, consider a perfectly competitive firm that uses labour as an input. The firm faces a market price of $10 for each unit of its output.

The total product, marginal product, and marginal revenue product that the firm receives from hiring 1 to 5 workers are reported in Table 12-1.

Table 12-1   Marginal Revenue Product of Labour

Labour input (workers)	Total product (number of goods)	Marginal product of labour	Marginal revenue product of labour
0	0	—	—
1	9	9	$90
2	17	8	80
3	22	5	50
4	25	3	30
5	26	1	10

The marginal revenue product of each additional worker is found by multiplying the marginal product of each additional worker by the market price of $10. The marginal revenue product of labour is the additional revenue that the firm earns from hiring an additional worker; it represents the **wage** that the firm is *willing* to pay for each additional worker. The wage that the firm *actually* pays is the **market wage rate,** which is determined by the **market demand** and **market supply of labour.** In a perfectly competitive *labour* market, the individual firm is a **wage-taker;** it takes the market wage rate as given, just as the firm in a perfectly competitive product market takes the price for its output as given. The market wage rate in a perfectly competitive labour market represents the firm's **marginal cost of labour,** the amount the firm must pay for each additional worker that it hires.

The perfectly competitive firm's profit-maximizing labour-demand decision is to hire workers up to the point where the marginal revenue product of the last worker hired is *just equal* to the market wage rate, which is the marginal cost of this last worker. For example, if the market wage rate is $50 per worker per day, the firm—whose marginal revenue product of labour is given in Table 12-1—would choose to hire 3 workers each day.

The firm's labour demand curve. The firm's profit-maximizing labour-demand decision is depicted graphically in Figure 12-1.

Figure 12-1 A perfectly competitive firm's profit-maximizing labour-demand decision

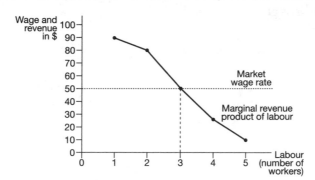

This figure graphs the marginal revenue product of labour data from Table 12-1 along with the market wage rate of $50. When the marginal revenue product of labour is graphed, it represents **the firm's labour demand curve.** The demand curve is downward sloping due to the law of diminishing returns; as more workers are hired, the marginal product of labor begins declining, causing the marginal revenue product of labour to fall as well. The intersection of the marginal revenue product curve with the market wage determines the number of workers that the firm hires, in this case 3 workers.

An individual's supply of labour. An individual's supply of labour depends on his or her **preferences** for two types of "goods": **consumption goods** and **leisure.** Consumption goods include all the goods that can be purchased with the income that an individual earns from working. Leisure is the good that individuals consume when they are not working. By working more (supplying more labour), an individual reduces his or her consumption of leisure but is able to increase his or her purchases of consumption goods.

In choosing between leisure and consumption, the individual faces two constraints. First, the individual is limited to twenty-four hours per day for work or leisure. Second, the individual's income from work is limited by the market *wage* rate that the individual receives for his or her labour skills. In a perfectly competitive labour market, workers—like firms—are **wage-takers;** they take the market wage rate that they receive as given.

An individual's labour supply curve. An example of an individual's labour supply curve is given in Figure 12-2.

Figure 12-2   An individual's labour supply curve

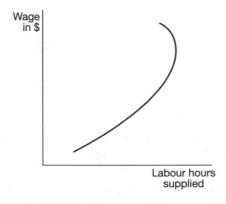

As wages increase, so does the **opportunity cost of leisure.** As leisure becomes more costly, workers tend to substitute more work hours for fewer leisure hours in order to consume the relatively cheaper consumption goods, which is the **substitution effect** of a higher wage.

An **income effect** is also associated with a higher wage. A higher wage leads to higher real incomes, provided that prices of consumption goods remain constant. As real incomes rise, individuals will demand more leisure, which is considered a **normal good**—the higher an individual's income, the easier it is for that individual to take more time off from work and still maintain a high standard of living in terms of consumption goods.

The substitution effect of higher wages tends to dominate the income effect at low wage levels, while the income effect of higher wages tends to dominate the substitution effect at high wage levels. The dominance of the income effect over the substitution effect at high wage levels is what accounts for the **backward-bending shape** of the individual's labour supply curve.

Market demand and supply of labour. Many different markets for labour exist, one for every **type** and **skill level** of labour. For example, the labour market for entry level accountants is different from the labour market for tennis pros. The demand for labour in a particular market— called the **market demand** for labour—is the amount of labour that *all* the firms participating in that market will demand at different market wage levels. The **market demand curve** for a particular type of labour is the horizontal summation of the marginal revenue product of labour curves of every firm in the market for that type of labour. The **market supply of labour** is the number of workers of a particular type and skill level who are willing to supply their labour to firms at different wage levels. The **market supply curve** for a particular type of labour is the horizontal summation of the individuals' labour supply curves. Unlike an individual's supply curve, the market supply curve *is not backward bending* because there will always be some workers in the market who will be willing to supply more labour and take less leisure time, even at relatively high wage levels.

Equilibrium in a Perfectly Competitive Market

While each labour market is different, the equilibrium market wage rate and the equilibrium number of workers employed in every *perfectly competitive labour market* is determined in the same manner: by *equating* the market demand for labour with the market supply of labour. The determination of equilibrium market wage and employment is illustrated in Figure 12-3.

Figure 12-3 Equilibrium in a perfectly competitive labour market

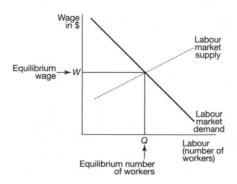

The equilibrium market wage is W, and the equilibrium number of workers employed is Q. At **wage rates** greater than W, the demand for labour would be less than the supply of labour, implying that there would be **a labour surplus.** At wage rates below W, the demand for labour would be greater than the supply of labour, implying that there would be a **labour shortage.** A labour surplus is eliminated when some workers agree to sell their labour for lower wages, thereby driving down the market wage rate to W. A labour shortage is eliminated when some firms agree to employ workers at higher wages, thereby driving the market wage rate up to W. At the equilibrium wage rate, there is no surplus or shortage of labour.

Labour Demand and Supply in a Monopsony

A labour market in which there is only one firm demanding labour is called a **monopsony.** The single firm in the market is referred to as the **monopsonist.** An example of a monopsony would be the only firm in a "company town," where the workers all work for that single firm.

Wage-searching behaviour. Because the monopsonist is the sole demander of labour in the market, the monopsonist's demand for labour is the **market demand for labour.** The supply of labour that the monopsonist faces is the **market supply of labour.** Unlike a firm operating in a perfectly competitive labour market, the monopsonist does not simply hire all the workers that it wants at the equilibrium market wage. The monopsonist faces the *upward-sloping* market supply curve; it is a **wage-searcher** rather than a **wage-taker.** If the monopsonist wants to increase the number of workers that it hires, it must increase the wage that it pays to *all* of its workers, including those whom it currently employs. The monopsonist's **marginal cost of hiring** an additional worker, therefore, will not be equal to the wage paid to that worker because the monopsonist will have to increase the wage that it pays to all of its workers.

A numerical example of a monopsony market is provided in Table 12-2. The first two columns provide data on the market supply of labour that the monopsonist faces. The third column reports the total cost to the monopsonist of hiring each worker, which is just the wage times the number of workers. The fourth column reports the marginal cost of labour, which is the change in monopsonist's total cost of labour as it hires additional workers.

Table 12-2   A Monopolist's Marginal Cost of Labour

Labour (number of workers)	Wage (per hour)	Total cost of labour	Marginal cost of labour
1	$10	$10	$10
2	15	30	20
3	20	60	30
4	25	100	40
5	30	150	50

Suppose the monopsonist wants to increase the number of workers that it hires from 2 to 3. In order to attract the third worker, the monopsonist must offer an hourly wage of $20 instead of $15. However, because the monopsonist cannot discriminate among its workers (and risk alienating them), it must offer the higher $20 wage to its two current employees. Hence, the monopsonist's costs from hiring the third worker are $60 (3 x $20), and the marginal cost from hiring the third worker is $30 ($60 – $30). The marginal cost of $30 exceeds the new market wage of $20 because the monopsonist must also pay its two current employees an hourly wage that is $5 higher than before.

Equilibrium in a Monopsony Market

In a monopsony market, the monopsonist firm—like any profit-maximizing firm—determines the equilibrium number of workers to hire by equating its marginal revenue product of labour with its marginal cost of labour. Figure 12-4 illustrates the monopsony labour market equilibrium, using the supply and cost data from Table 12-2.

The marginal revenue product of labour equals the marginal cost of labour when the firm employs 3 workers. The equilibrium market wage rate is determined by the market labour supply curve. In order to employ 3 workers, the firm will have to pay a wage of $20. Hence, the equilibrium wage is $20, and the equilibrium number of workers employed is 3.

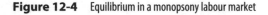

Figure 12-4   Equilibrium in a monopsony labour market

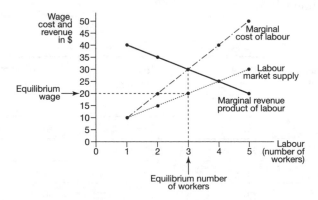

Because the monopsonist is the only demander of labour in the market, it has the power to pay wages *below* the **marginal revenue product of labour** and to hire *fewer workers* than a perfectly competitive firm. In Figure 12-4, the perfectly competitive firm would face a market wage of $25 because that is the wage rate corresponding to the intersection of the market demand and supply curves. If the perfectly competitive firm had the same marginal revenue product as the monopsonist, the perfectly competitive firm would equate marginal revenue product with the market wage and choose to hire 4 workers at $25. The monopsonist's decision to hire only 3 workers at a wage of $20 makes it clear that monopsony, like monopoly in a product market, *reduces* society's welfare.

Chapter 13

CAPITAL MARKET

Capital goods are **input goods** that are purchased in order to increase the production of future output. Capital goods include **tangible goods,** such as buildings and structures, machinery and equipment, and inventories of goods in process. Capital goods also include **intangible goods** such as franchises, literary rights, and product brand names. An individual's investment in knowledge from taking classes or learning "on the job" is another form of intangible capital called human capital. This section considers the market for all kinds of capital goods.

Measures of Capital

While labour is measured in terms of the number of workers hired or the number of hours worked, it is difficult to measure **capital** in terms of physical units because there are so many different types of capital goods. Capital goods, therefore, are simply measured in terms of their **market** or **dollar value.**

Capital stock. The market value of capital goods at a *given point in time,* for example, at the end of a year, is referred to as the **capital stock.** A firm's capital stock is the market value of its factory, equipment, and other capital goods at a given point in time. A household's capital stock is the market value of its residential structures, human capital, and other capital goods at a given point in time. Firms' and households' capital stocks will vary over time due to **investment** and **depreciation.**

Investment. Investment is the addition of new capital goods to a firm's or household's capital stock. Investment is a **flow measurement;** it represents the market value of new capital purchased or produced *per unit of time.* For example, if a firm with $90,000 in capital at the end of last year purchases $10,000 in capital during the current year, its investment for this year is $10,000, while its capital stock at the end of the current year is $100,000.

Depreciation. Depreciation is also a flow measurement; it measures the reduction in market value of a firm's or household's capital stock per unit of time. Depreciation of the capital stock is caused by normal wear and tear and by the obsolescence of capital goods over time.

When depreciation over a period of time *exceeds* investment over the same period of time, the capital stock *decreases;* otherwise, the capital stock *increases* or *remains the same.* For example, if the firm with $90,000 in capital at the end of last year purchases $10,000 in new capital during the current year, but experiences $20,000 in depreciation during the current year, its capital stock at the end of the current year will have *decreased* to $80,000 ($90,000 + $10,000 − $20,000). If depreciation during the current year is *only* $5,000, instead of $20,000, then the firm's capital stock at the end of the current year will have *increased* to $95,000.

Capital, Loanable Funds, and the Interest Rate

The demand and supply for different types of **capital** take place in **capital markets.** In these capital markets, firms are typically **demanders of capital,** while households are typically **suppliers of capital.** Households supply capital goods *indirectly,* by choosing to *save* a portion of their incomes and lending these savings to banks. Banks, in turn, lend household savings to firms that use these funds to purchase capital goods.

Loanable funds. The term *loanable funds* is used to describe funds that are available for borrowing. Loanable funds consist of household savings and/or bank loans. Because investment in new capital goods is frequently made with loanable funds, the demand and supply of capital is often discussed in terms of the demand and supply of loanable funds.

Interest rate. The interest rate is the cost of demanding or borrowing loanable funds. Alternatively, the interest rate is the rate of return from supplying or lending loanable funds. The interest rate is typically measured as an **annual percentage rate.** For example, a firm that borrows $20,000 in funds for one year, at an annual interest rate of 5%, will have to repay the lender $21,000 at the end of the year; this amount includes the $20,000 borrowed plus $1,000 in interest ($20,000 x .05).

If the firm borrows $20,000 for two years at an annual interest rate of 5%, it will have to repay the lender $22,050 at the end of two years. After one year, the firm will owe the lender $21,000 as explained above; however, because the loan is for two years, the firm does not have to repay the lender until the end of the second year. During the second year, the firm is charged **compound interest,** which means it is charged interest on both the **principal** of $20,000 and the **accumulated unpaid interest** of $1,000. It is as though the firm receives a new loan at the beginning of the second year for $21,000. Thus, at the end of the second year, the firm repays the lender $21,000 + (21,000 x .05) = $22,050.

In general, the amount that has to be repaid on a loan of X dollars for t years at an annual interest rate of r is given by the formula

$$\text{amount repaid} = X(1 + r)^t$$

For example, if X = $20,000, r = .05, and t = 2, the amount repaid is found to be $20,000 x $(1.05)^2$ = $22,050.

Determination of the equilibrium interest rate. The **equilibrium interest rate** is determined in the loanable funds market. All lenders and borrowers of loanable funds are participants in the loanable funds market. The total amount of funds supplied by lenders makes up the supply of loanable funds, while the total amount of funds demanded by borrowers makes up the demand for loanable funds. The loanable funds market is illustrated in Figure 13-1. The demand curve for loanable funds is downward sloping, indicating that at lower interest rates borrowers will demand more funds for investment. The supply curve for loanable funds is upward sloping, indicating that at higher interest rates lenders are willing to lend more funds to investors. The equilibrium interest rate is determined by the intersection of the demand and supply curves for loanable funds, as indicated in Figure 13-1.

Figure 13-1 Determination of the equilibrium interest rate

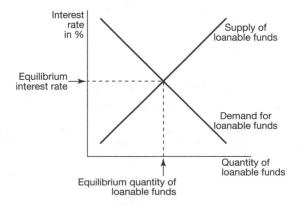

Rate of return on capital and the demand for loanable funds. The **demand for loanable funds** takes account of the **rate of return on capital.** The rate of return on capital is the additional revenue that a firm can earn from its employment of new capital. This additional revenue is usually measured as a percentage rate per unit of time, which is why it is called the *rate* of return on capital. Firms will demand loanable funds as long as the rate of return on capital is greater than or equal to the interest rate paid on funds borrowed. If capital becomes more productive—that is, if the rate of return on capital *increases*—the demand curve for loanable funds depicted in Figure 13-1 will shift out and to the right, causing the equilibrium interest rate to rise, *ceteris paribus.*

Thriftiness and the supply of loanable funds. The **supply of loanable funds** reflects the **thriftiness** of households and other lenders. If households become more thrifty—that is, if households decide to *save more*—the supply of loanable funds *increases.* The increase in the supply of loanable funds shifts the supply curve for loanable funds depicted in Figure 13-1 down and to the right, causing the equilibrium interest rate to fall, *ceteris paribus.*

Present Value and Investment Decisions

Firms purchase capital goods to increase their future output and income. Income earned in the future is often evaluated in terms of its **present value.** The present value of future income is the value of having this future income today.

Present value formula. The present value of receiving $20,000 one year from now can be calculated using the **present value formula.** The formula for finding the present value of X dollars received t years from now at the current market interest rate r is

$$\text{present value} = \frac{\$X}{(1 + r)^t}$$

For example, if $X = \$20,000$, $t = 1$, and $r = .05$, the present value of $20,000 received *one* year from now is $20,000/(1.05)^1 = \$19,047.62$.

The present value of $20,000 received *two* years from now at an interest rate of 5% is found by setting $X = \$20,000$, $t = 2$, and $r = .05$. The present value in this case is $\$20,000/(1.05)^2 = \$18,140.59$. As you can see from these examples, the present value of the future income is the amount of income that you would need to invest today, at current market interest rates, in order to obtain the same amount of future income at the same future date.

Firm's investment decision. The **firm's investment decision** is to determine whether to purchase new capital. In determining whether to purchase new capital—for example, new equipment—the firm will take into account the *price* of the new equipment, the *revenue* that the new equipment will generate for the firm *over time,* and the *scrap value* of the new equipment. The firm will also take into account the interest rate, which represents the firm's opportunity cost of investing in the new equipment. It will use the interest rate to calculate the present value of the future net income that it expects to earn from its purchase of the new capital equipment. If the present value is *positive,* the firm will choose to purchase the new equipment. If the present value is *negative,* it is better off forgoing the investment in new equipment.

An example. As an example, consider a restaurant that is trying to decide whether to invest in a new piece of capital equipment—a jukebox. The jukebox costs $7,000 and lasts 4 years. The restaurant estimates that the jukebox will provide it with income of $2,000 per year, net of maintenance costs. After 4 years, the scrap value of the jukebox is estimated at $500. In determining whether to purchase the jukebox, the firm will calculate the net present value of the present and future income that it receives from purchasing the jukebox. The firm's present value calculations are shown in Table 13-1 for an interest rate of 10%.

Table 13-1   Present Value of Jukebox at an Interest Rate of 10%

Year	Outlay (–) or income	Present value calculation	Present value of outlay (–) or income
0	–$7,000	—	–$7,000
1	2,000	$2,000/(1.10)1	1,818
2	2,000	2,000/(0.10)2	1,653
3	2,000	2,000/(1.10)3	1,503
4	2,500	2,500/(1.10)4	1,708
		Total net present value:	$318

The calculation of *net* present value includes the initial outlay of $7,000 for the jukebox. The present value formula is used to calculate the present value of the $2,000 annual income received in each of the 4 years. In the fourth year, the $500 scrap value is added to the $2,000 in income received from the jukebox. The total net present value of the jukebox turns out to be –$318. Because this amount is negative, the firm will choose to forgo purchasing the jukebox.

As Table 13-1 reveals, the firm's net present value calculations depend on the interest rate. The higher the interest rate is, the higher the firm's opportunity cost of investing in the jukebox. A higher interest rate lowers the present value of the future income earned from capital, making it less profitable for the firm to invest in new capital; however, if interest rates fall, the opportunity cost of investing in new capital also falls. The lower the interest rate is, the higher the present value of the future income earned from new capital investment, and the more likely it is that firms will invest in new capital.

For example, consider what happens to the firm's net present value calculations for the jukebox when the interest rate *falls* from 10% to 6%. Table 13-2 repeats the present value calculations of Table 13-1 at the lower interest rate of 6%.

Table 13-2   Present Value of Jukebox at an Interest Rate of 6%

Year	Outlay (–) or income	Present value calculation	Present value of outlay (–) or income
0	–$7,000	—	–$7,000
1	2,000	$2,000/(1.06)1	1,887
2	2,000	2,000/(1.06)2	1,780
3	2,000	2,000/(1.06)4	1,679
4	2,500	2,500/(1.06)4	1,980
		Total net present value:	$326

At the lower interest rate, the net present value of the jukebox is positive ($326). If the firm can obtain $7,000 in loanable funds at 6% interest, it will choose to purchase the jukebox.

The decision to invest in other types of capital goods can also be made on the basis of present value calculations. For example, the decision to invest in human capital by attending college is based on the present value of the future income that an individual can earn with a college degree. If the present value is positive, the individual will choose to attend college. If the present value is negative, the individual will not attend college and will perhaps take a job instead.